TABLE OF CONTENTS

LIST OF FIGURES

THIS PAGE INTENTIONALLY LEFT BLANK

LIST OF TABLES

LIST OF ACRONYMS AND ABBREVIATIONS

ACLU	American Civil Liberties Union
APA	American Psychological Association
AQAP	Al Qaeda in the Arabian Peninsula
ATF	Bureau of Alcohol, Tobacco and Firearms
BOP	Bureau of Prisons
CVE	Countering Violent Extremism
DEA	Drug Enforcement Administration
DNI	Director of National Intelligence
DOJ	Department of Justice
DRO	Office of Detention and Removal
FATA	Federally Administered Tribal Areas
FBI	Federal Bureau of Investigation
FOIA	Freedom of Information Act
FOUO	For Official Use Only
HRF	Human Rights First
IACP	International Association of Chiefs of Police
INSA	Intelligence and National Security Alliance
JTTF	Joint Terrorism Task Force
KSM	Khalid Sheikh Mohammed
NIMBY	Not in My Backyard
NYPD	New York Police Department
OVC	Office for Victims of Crime
QIASS	Qatar International Academy for Security Studies
RRG	Religious Rehabilitation Group
START	Study of Terrorism and Responses to Terrorism

I. INTRODUCTION: THE TERRORIST'S REENTRY

Terrorism is… specifically designed
to have far reaching psychological effects
beyond the immediate victim(s)
or object of the terrorist attack.

– Bruce Hoffman, 2006, p. 40

A. PROBLEM STATEMENT

How "far" terrorism's reach stretches is difficult to determine. Extensive research has been done to examine the variety of consequences caused by a terrorist act, including political, economic, legal, and social to name a few. However, does the deleterious effect of a terrorist subside once he is captured, convicted, imprisoned, and freed into society? On the other hand, is there opportunity for his vision to endure or his work to continue?

Clear evidence demonstrates that those convicted of terrorism-related crimes have a greater likelihood of leaving prison one day than remaining indefinitely exiled from free society. This may sound counter-intuitive, as those convicted of more extreme cases receive the most stringent penalties. However, there is a growing population of individuals who have been convicted of a terrorism-related crime in an American court, and have already—or will soon—walk free, just as a common criminal convicted for burglary or assault would.

This is not to be mistaken for those who may radicalize while serving time in prison. Extensive literature has been written about whether prisons are incubators for new terrorists. Theories are emerging that challenge widespread claims that criminals are even becoming terrorists in prison. A CRS Report for Congress states:

> The lack of conclusive prison-based radicalization among the jihadist terrorism plots and foiled attacks since 9/11 suggests that the threat emanating from prisons does not seem as substantial as some experts may fear. (Bjelopera & Randol, 2010, p. 22)

Such a suggestion makes examining those who have already been associated with a terrorism-related crime that much more critical. Therefore, we have examined those already named as terrorists by the judicial system. According to a 2009 Human Rights

1

First report, only eleven of 171 defendants received a life sentence for international terrorism connected to Islamist extremist terrorist organizations (Zabel & Benjamin, 2009, p. 9). Conversely, the remaining 160 of the 171 individuals have the opportunity to walk free, as their average term of imprisonment is fewer than nine years, and their median term of imprisonment is fewer than five years (Zabel & Benjamin, 2009, p. 9). Among these 160 convicts are popularly recognized names, such as "American Talib" John Walker Lindh, who was sentenced to 20 years in prison (Johnson, 2009) in 2002, and suspected dirty bomb plotter Jose Padilla, who was sentenced to 17 years (Whoriskey & Eggen, 2008) in 2008. Both are relatively young men who will likely have time ahead of them when they are freed from prison.[1] Also included are representatives from the sensationalized Lackawanna Six and Portland Seven terror plots, as well as others who have participated in conspiracy to murder persons overseas, provided material support to foreign terrorist organizations, or perjured themselves and obstructed justice. Some have been released already, while others will be released in the not-too-distant future.

Yet the narrative about these figures tapers off once a verdict is reached and a prison sentence is issued. This is both a blessing and a curse. On one hand, it is fortunate that the United States has not had to reactively deal with the release of a convicted terrorist from prison. However, on the other hand, the nation may be failing to address proactively a potential threat stream.

The author of this thesis argues that the field of terrorism studies is limited in its examination of what Jeremy Travis, former director of the National Institute of Justice, calls the "iron law of imprisonment: they all come back" (J. Travis, 2006, p. xvii). He adds:

> Reentry is the process of leaving prison and returning to society. Reentry is not a form of supervision… Reentry is not a goal, like rehabilitation or reintegration. Reentry is not an option. (J. Travis, 2006, p. xxi)

---

[1] Lindh will be 41 years old and Padilla will be 55 years old when released from prison in 2022 and 2025, respectively.

Simply stated, reentry happens. Americans may generally have internalized Travis's iron law for more common criminals, but the present research finds that such an awareness does not extend to those associated with terrorism. As Michael Jacobson of the Washington Institute for Near East Policy states, "(t)here is growing recognition that capturing or killing every terrorist is not a realistic strategy" (Jacobson, 2010, p. 1).

B. RESEARCH QUESTIONS

Therefore, we[2] set out to learn more about this frontier of the terrorism continuum by investigating:

- what ripple effects are generated by the release of a convicted terrorist into a host American population, and

- what issues America should consider after releasing someone convicted of terrorism-related crimes.

C. FINDINGS AND IMPLICATIONS

The poem, "Drop a Pebble in the Water" (Fellman, 1936) by James W. Foley (1874–1939), provides a metaphor for the phenomena and relationships in our inquiry:

Drop a pebble in the water: just a splash and it is gone;
But there's half-a-hundred ripples circling on and on and on,
Spreading, spreading, from the center, flowing on out to sea.
And there is no way of telling where the end is going to be.

Just as a pebble dropped in the water causes "ripples circling on and on," a convicted terrorist released into American communities may cause ripples circling on and on. Additionally, since "there is no way of telling where the end is going to be," this research is designed to begin that discussion.

The immediate set of ripples (and most evident one) is directly related to the terrorist and what he does.[3] This includes things to do with the justice system and

---

[2] The term 'we' represents the author of this thesis, along with the thesis committee, and the voice of an emerging, collective dialogue that this author intends to initiate. The opinions expressed within this document solely represent the opinions of the author and should not be considered as an official position of the U.S. Government or the Naval Postgraduate School.

[3] Evidence has shown that terrorists are both male and female. For writing purposes, the individual terrorist will be listed as a male.

3

restriction of his movement or freedoms. Separate from the direct actions of the terrorist, however, is the collection of rings that may be examined to assess if those "little waves a-flowing to a great big wave have grown." Understanding victims, neighbors, activists, and other stakeholders in the community that receives a convicted terrorist may provide insight into who is affected by his release and broader societal issues of concern. By looking first at the terrorist and second at the community he (re)joins, our expectation was to begin understanding the type, size, and breadth of these ripples.

Despite an extensive effort to identify the locations of convicted and released terrorists and to assess the assumed ripples around them, our search was futile. This left us with an evidentiary black hole. We had hypothesized so much in the beginning about what we might expect to see in the United States when one of these people got out of prison. However, we were bequeathed with nothing. We found no ripple effects because we found no terrorists.

From this fact and the subsequent analysis surrounding it, we construed four primary findings: (1) we do not know if convicted and released terrorists present a threat; (2) convicted terrorists are treated no differently from most convicted criminals; (3) the American public knows very little about convicted and released terrorists; (4) there is no defined entity responsible for convicted and released terrorists. The implications drawn from each of these findings bolster many issues for America's consideration after releasing a convicted terrorist. Should we simply maintain the status quo? How can risk be gauged to determine whether or not an individual should be freed? Can detainment be extended beyond a court-issued prison sentence? Does the public registry model used to monitor sex offenders have applicability for convicted terrorists upon their release into society?

Many entities are directly and indirectly vested in the answers to these questions. As the United States has learned since 9/11, there are social, political, military, economic, and diplomatic consequences that follow whatever action *or inaction* is taken in response to homeland security matters. Therefore, failure to examine the issue further could have cascading effects in the years ahead. It is essential that the homeland security and justice communities, including analysts, policy makers, investigators, judges, attorneys, prison

4

officials, and probation officers collaborate to examine the implications of this issue. Further, academics and practitioners from social sciences, such as psychology and sociology, as well as those in the fields of history, law, political science, public policy, communications, and social work serve an important role in determining how to address this next phase of the terrorism continuum. This is an interdisciplinary issue that requires what Gerencser, Van Lee, Napolitano, and Kelly (hereafter, "Gerencser et al.") call a "megacommunity" (Gerencser et al., 2008) to facilitate the discourse.

The unique aspect of this segment of terrorism research is that it has a predictable timeline. We do not know when the next cell will spawn or how the next attack will strike. Unlike our limited knowledge about how long the United States will be in Afghanistan or what nebulous expectations were held following the removal of Saddam Hussein from power in Iraq, we definitively know when convicted terrorists complete their prison sentences (N. Lipana, personal communication, June 24, 2010). Therefore, for as unpredictable as terrorism is, the release of a terrorist from prison is a marked event that can be leveraged to address a potential threat. As Travis opines, "(t)here is something irrational about a criminal justice system that spends ten times as much on a prisoner's last day in prison as it does on his first day after prison (J. Travis, 2006, p. 334). For this reason, we must begin to explore possible options for the future and the impact of implementing those options, especially for those associated with acts of terrorism.

D.   OVERVIEW OF UPCOMING CHAPTERS

This thesis is divided into six parts. Chapter II contextualizes the key requirement of our discussion: who is a convicted and released terrorist in America. The paths of a captured terrorist are mapped out to differentiate what this research is and, importantly, what it is not. This section looks at nominally related datasets, such as Guantánamo Bay detainees, those sentenced to life in prison, and those departing the United States. These lanes offer significant opportunity for future research as the universe of captured terrorists continues to grow. Chapter II also features a literature review that introduces various angles for exploration about convicted and released terrorists and the ripples felt by government both domestically and internationally, by the individual himself, and by the communities he touches. The literature review covers deportation, sentencing guidelines, post-prison supervision requirements, terrorist rehabilitation, recidivism, travel restrictions, political ramifications, and effects on victims.

Chapter III describes where our quest began and maps out the rigorous journey to our findings. This thesis traveled many paths, and this section is designed to introduce where it originated: its theoretical and methodological foundations, hypotheses, case selection, and initial set of research parameters.

Chapter IV explains the assembly line that a captured terrorist is likely to experience in the federal court system, from law enforcement through prison and supervised release, and subsequent freedom. This analysis allows us to draw lines that connect what we know with what we need to know on the next phase of the terrorism continuum.

Chapter V and Chapter VI expand upon our four core findings and their implications, and weigh the pros and cons of possible courses of action. These sections also revisit the scholarly literature in an effort to discern and understand the effects of an individual on society, as well as the effects of society on the individual. The implications discussion is an introduction to what scholars, practitioners, and policy makers may expect when faced with future decisions about the ripples caused by a convicted and released terrorist in America.

In Chapter VII, we appraise the concept of the "megacommunity," and notionally apply its tenets to the issue of convicted and released terrorists. We discuss some of the critical elements required to stimulate an emerging discourse in terrorism scholarship, as well as future public policy.

While a sense of urgency does not currently exist on this matter, recognition of the issue is a crucial first step. Two of al Qaeda's "founding fathers," Sheik Omar Abdel Rahman (responsible for planning the bombing of the World Trade Center in 1993) and Ayman al-Zawahiri (Osama bin Laden's "number two") were imprisoned for planning the assassination of Egyptian president Anwar Sadat, and subsequently released. Was the ideology for the current al Qaeda movement developed in prison? Has their influence been greater since prison? Similarly, could another ideologue be forged in American prisons today, to be released tomorrow?

Convicted terrorists have already been released from American prisons, and more are scheduled for release in the years ahead. Are terrorists like all other criminals? Are their crimes more egregious, influential, or dangerous than others? How great is their risk to society once they are freed? Are the tools of Western culture sufficient to deal with terrorism-related crimes? Our responsibilities are to critically examine the ripple effects created by convicted and released terrorists and the suitability of existing mechanisms, as well as to creatively explore what actions may be required in the future.

THIS PAGE INTENTIONALLY LEFT BLANK

II. BACKGROUND: ESTABLISHING A FRAMEWORK

Accuracy is not at stake so much
as establishing the structural boundaries of a fact:
where is the accurate description?

– Glaser & Strauss, 1967, p. 24

To understand the place of the convicted and released terrorists in America, it is helpful to define them, and to survey the environment where they exist. The difficulty in performing such an exercise is that all of the policies, theories, strategies, and literature connected to the subject intertwine and overlap into a countless array of perspectives that can only be fully absorbed through subject matter immersion. Much has been written about planning and operational terrorists before they are captured, including radicalization, recruitment, cell organization, financing, training, and tactics. However, less is known further along the continuum when terrorists are captured, convicted, and eventually released from prison.

Thus, this chapter is an attempt to draw conceptual boundaries, pave a lane, and establish a basic framework. We will first explain what defines a terrorist. Next, we will map the various paths of the imprisoned to maintain methodical and systematic discipline and to preempt inaccurate comparisons. Finally, we will look at some of the literature to validate our claim that the field of terrorism studies can broaden its knowledge base through further analysis of this subject.

A. WHAT IS TERRORISM?

Various interpretations exist as to how someone is labeled a terrorist or associated with an act of terrorism. Bruce Hoffman defines terrorism as:

> …the deliberate creation and exploitation of fear through violence in the pursuit of political change… specifically designed to have far-reaching psychological effects beyond the immediate victim(s) or object of the terrorist attack…. meant to instill fear within, and thereby intimidate, a wider 'target audience'… (T)errorists seek to obtain the leverage, influence, and power they otherwise lack to effect political change on either a local or international scale. (Hoffman, 2006, p. 40)

This may include a multitude of crimes. For purposes of our research, we are focused on those tried in civilian court, within the boundaries of our sovereign territory.[4] The U.S. Department of Justice (DOJ) National Security Division, in a summary of all terrorism convictions since 9/11, divides them into two groups: Category I cases are directly related to terrorism, while Category II cases include a variety of non-terrorism charges with a link to terrorism. Table 1 provides a more detailed summary.

Table 1.   Terrorism conviction categories (From: U.S. Department of Justice, National Security Division, 2010).

CATEGORY I	CATEGORY II
Category I cases involve violations of federal statutes that are directly related to international terrorism and that are utilized regularly in international terrorism matters.	Category II cases include defendants charged with violating a variety of other statutes where the investigation involved an identified link to international terrorism.
These statutes prohibit, for example, terrorist acts abroad against United States nationals, the use of weapons of mass destruction, conspiracy to murder persons overseas, providing material support to terrorists or foreign terrorist organizations, receiving military style training from foreign terrorist organizations, and bombings of public places or government facilities.	These Category II cases include offenses, such as those involving fraud, immigration, firearms, drugs, false statements, perjury, and obstruction of justice, as well as general conspiracy charges under 18 U.S.C. § 371.

On one level, the classification of the crime is less important to the present research than the path taken by the individual after being captured and placed into the system. As long as he is convicted of what DOJ sees as a terrorism-related crime, what is of interest here is the ripple effect caused by his release from prison into American society.

---

[4] The United States has yet to fully resolve whether military or civilian courts provide the better place for a terrorist to receive his judgment. Our research will focus on those tried in civilian court, with a dataset provided by Human Rights First. Further details on the dataset are described in the Methodology chapter.

On another level, though, the nature or classification of the crime is relevant to us because it enables an investigation into whether convicted terrorists are or should be treated indistinguishably from other convicted criminals, socially or legally. A terrorist pursues a political agenda that threatens national security in a way that most other criminals do not. This does not trivialize the impact or cost of other crime; rather, it introduces the predicate that serves as the central difference between a "street" crime and a terrorist crime: a terrorist crime is a national security offense that has wider implications. In a report published by the International Centre for the Study of Radicalisation and Political Violence, Peter Neumann (2010) makes the argument for differentiation between terrorists and other criminals:

> Even today, most criminal justice systems recognise—sometimes explicitly—that individuals charged with or convicted of terrorism related offences are different from 'ordinary' criminals. They are investigated by special sections of the police forces and brought to court by special prosecutors. The laws under which they are charged—anti-terrorism laws—were created specifically for them, and the courts at which they stand trial are special (or specialised) courts. This—governments argue—reflects the particularly serious nature of their crimes, which are directed against the state and society as a whole. Yet it also demonstrates that the idea of 'criminalising' and 'de-politicising' terrorist offences—if taken seriously and fully internalised—is contradictory at best, and may in fact prevent prison authorities from developing a sophisticated understanding of the particular challenges posed by politically motivated offenders, including terrorists, in prison. (p. 14)

Neumann further asserts that this differentiation lays the groundwork for discussing what prison regime is acceptable for terrorist detainees. Our attention expands this narrative even further along the terrorism continuum—and asks what can be learned *following* their release from prison, whether we have a sophisticated understanding of the challenges posed by convicted and released terrorists, and whether they are handled, in principle or in practice, differently from 'ordinary' criminals.

11

B.   PATHS OF THE IMPRISONED

Mapping the routes that an alleged or actual terrorist may follow upon incarceration can help us extrapolate to the unique space our research occupies. By establishing such a framework, the intention is not to explore each path rigorously, but rather to reduce confusion by separating what this research is from what it is not.

For example, the expert bomb maker for al Qaeda in the Arabian Peninsula (AQAP), Ibrahim Hassan Al Asiri, completed jail time in Saudi Arabia (Yemen Parcel Bombmaker, 2010). He was supposedly behind the attempted bombings of Northwest Flight 253 (also known as the Christmas Day 'underwear bomber') in 2009 and air cargo shipments from Yemen in 2010. However, he was not captured in the United States, he was not convicted in a U.S. court, he did not spend prison time in the United States, and he did not remain in America after his release. Therefore, he would not be a subject for our study.

Displaying a visual model has its limitations (for example, it does not address the appeals process and other detailed judicial procedures), but it can be used nonetheless as a starting point for future scholarship, as the broader population is understood in the future. Figure 1 depicts a composite summary of the terrain for the captured terrorist. The remainder of the section briefly describes the alternative pathways of the individual through the system.

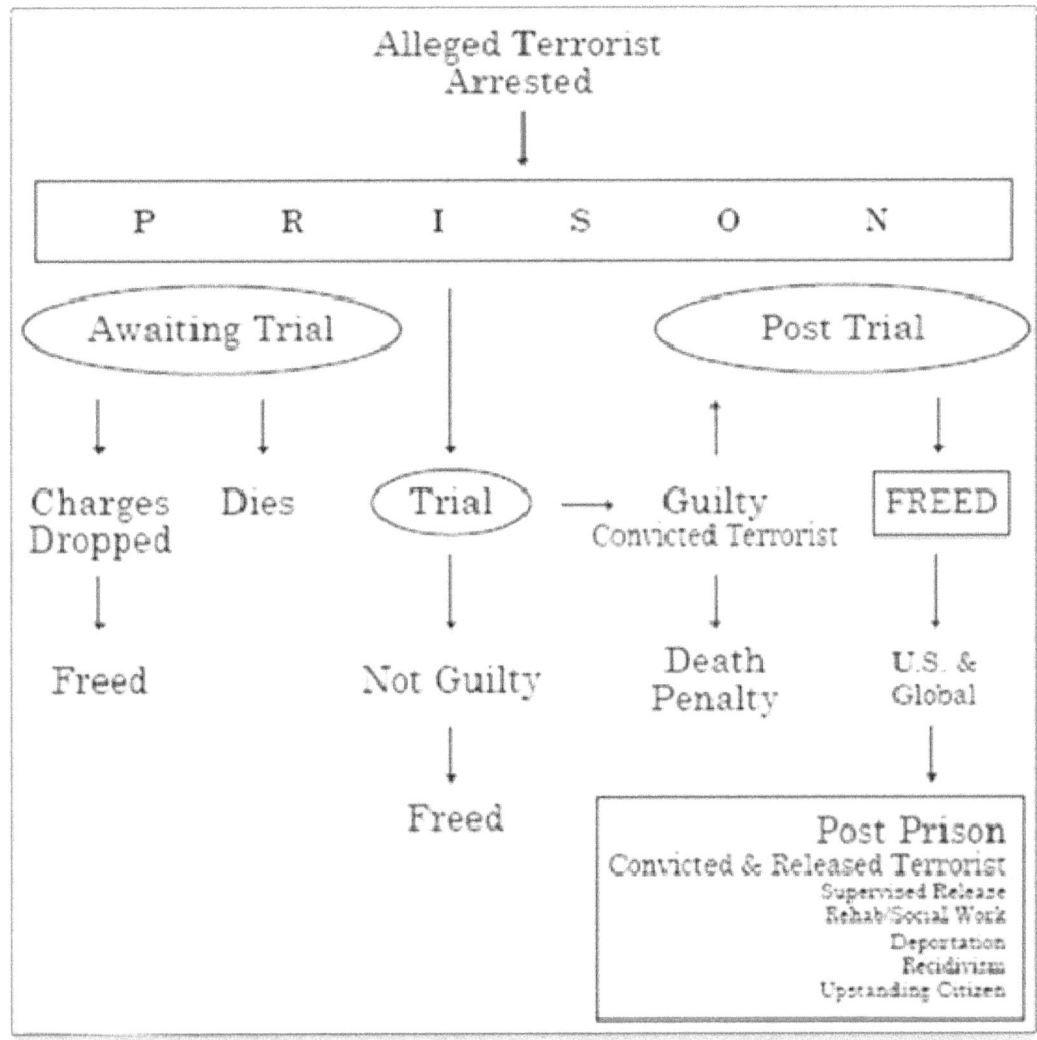

Figure 1.   The paths of the imprisoned

1.   Alleged Terrorist Is Arrested

To begin and repeat, classification of the offense is not central to this research, so long as it is terrorism-related. "Terrorists" for this study include the complete universe of those participating in any role associated with an attack. Examples are a strategist or planner, a front-line operator, such as a bomb maker or the handler of a suicide bomber, or an individual who provides shelter for or funding to a particular individual, organization, or cause. Any of the aforementioned actions is grounds for arrest and imprisonment. We call them "alleged" terrorists because their guilt has not yet been determined through the judicial process.

2. Awaiting Trial

There is a variety of paths of people who could be followed in other research circumstances who might be relevant. For the sake of scoping, we concentrated on those actually convicted.

Some alleged and arrested terrorists have their charges dropped while awaiting trial, enabling them to notionally shed the "terrorist" designation and regain their freedom. They may be labeled "enemy combatants" until their status is clarified through the judicial process. For example, following the March 11, 2004 attacks on the Madrid rail system, an American citizen was incorrectly connected to the materials used in the bombings, and was imprisoned for two weeks (Eggen, 2006). This path has received great attention by civil liberties organizations to include the American Civil Liberties Union and Human Rights First (U.S.: Scores of Muslim Men Jailed Without Charge, 2005). Once released, some resume life outside the United States. In such cases, the individual may pursue one of two paths—to either re-enter the global community away from the terrorism business altogether, or to join the terrorist battle against America and its interests. The latter is often labeled as a recidivist released from the prison at Guantánamo Bay.

On the face of it, released Guantánamo detainees seem the best representative sample of an "ex-terrorist" population. However, the terminology used by the Office of the Director of National Intelligence (DNI), as described in Table 2, is telling.

Table 2.   DNI Categorization of Terrorists for Measurement of Recidivism (From: Office of the Director of National Intelligence, 2010)

Reporting Qualifications for "Confirmed"	Reporting Qualifications for "Suspected"
A preponderance of information identifying a specific former GTMO detainee as directly involved in terrorist or insurgent activities. For the purposes of this definition, engagement in anti-U.S. statements or propaganda does not qualify as terrorist or insurgent activity.	Plausible but unverified or single-source reporting indicating a specific former GTMO detainee is directly involved in terrorist or insurgent activities. For the purposes of this definition, engagement in anti-U.S. statements or propaganda does not qualify as terrorist or insurgent activity.

This population does not constitute a suitable data set because the legalities of how they are categorized and confirmed. Thus, it is incompatible with our baseline requirements for U.S. civilian trial and imprisonment. Additionally, a "preponderance of information" is not described, and while the categorization for confirmed terrorists is relatively stronger than that of suspected terrorists, there is no evidence of a conviction. Therefore, such a description of a "confirmed" terrorist may be premature. As an assistant professor of journalism at Northeastern University in Boston noted in 2009, "Others who had taken up terrorism upon being released from Guantánamo… may never have engaged in terrorist acts before their imprisonment" (Kennedy, 2009).

Regardless, most media and policymakers continue to use terms, such as "go back to terrorism," (How Many Detainees Go Back to Terrorism?, 2009) "return to the fight," (Mulrine, 2009) and "returning to militant activity," (Barnes & Parsons, 2010) when it has not yet been proven if they were terrorists in the first place, as seen in Figure 2. Some researchers have challenged the accuracy of recidivism data provided by the Department of Defense, seeking greater transparency (Bergen, Tiedemann, & Lebovich, 2011).

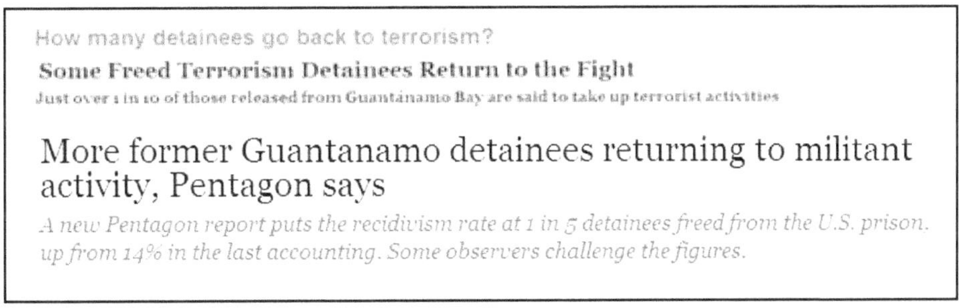

How many detainees go back to terrorism?
Some Freed Terrorism Detainees Return to the Fight
Just over 1 in 10 of those released from Guantánamo Bay are said to take up terrorist activities

More former Guantanamo detainees returning to militant activity, Pentagon says
A new Pentagon report puts the recidivism rate at 1 in 5 detainees freed from the U.S. prison, up from 14% in the last accounting. Some observers challenge the figures.

Figure 2.   Headlines on detainees choosing terrorism

Obviously, it will be relevant to know the influence and effects of imprisonment itself. When there is enough data, we can unravel the sometimes conflicting terminology used in various disciplines (i.e., what recidivism means, how radicalization is assessed). However, that is not yet completely clear in the scholarship. We are not investigating standards of evidence or the legality of crime categories; this would be another opportunity for further research to find out how confident we are in our labels and categories in the judicial process. Rather, we are assuming that if they were convicted, they were guilty. The population for our research focuses on those who have been proven through conviction to have been directly or indirectly involved in an act of terrorism.

As the debate continues in America about what to do with alleged terrorists upon their capture, some may remain jailed while awaiting trial for an indefinite period of time and die (by suicide or natural causes). While not directly related to our work, we are introducing this path as another path for future research. Death in detention may affect their reputation or legacy and require additional attention in the future.

3.   Trial

If the individual is not released before trial (or does not die awaiting trial), he will go to trial. There are three possible verdicts: not guilty, guilty verdict with death penalty, and guilty verdict with prison sentence. Our effort will *not* focus on the first two. If someone is judged not guilty, we assume as a society that we need not be (or have no legal right to be) concerned about him. There is already extensive debate about the longer-term consequences of executing a convicted terrorist (Eviatar, 2009). A death penalty sentence may cause ripple effects, but not due to the introduction of the ex-convict to society.

We are interested in the post-conviction, post-incarceration terrorist. This excludes the likes of Ramzi Yousef, Richard Reid, and Zacarias Moussaoui, each of whom will remain incarcerated for life. Our interest is in those who can be observed in public life, and not solely by a correctional officer. Whether or not he presents a greater threat than before his capture is not relevant; what is relevant is our ability to learn from him moving forward.

4.   Post-Trial (Post-Prison)

There are several reasons a convicted terrorist would be released from prison, including completion of the required term, political pardon, commutation of sentence, or amnesty. In some cases, the individual will depart the United States, either involuntarily through deportation, or voluntarily.

Like the individual released from jail before trial, the convicted terrorist may reenter the global community away from the terrorism business altogether, or reestablish contact with his prior social network. A return to terrorism and illicit activity would accurately count as recidivism. In fact, the prison experience may be seen as a rite of passage and provide an individual with the same "street credibility" that gangs or organized crime syndicates recognize as a positive attribute upon returning to his former home.

The convicted terrorist could also be sent to a rehabilitation program like those offered in Yemen, Saudi Arabia, and Singapore. Such an offering is designed to provide the positive reinforcements that keep him away from the terrorist's life and enable him to re-enter the global community as no threat to others. A summary of the Saudi program is as follows:

> The Saudi policy for tackling extremism and radicalization is outlined in a plan termed the PRAC strategy, which stands for Prevention, Rehabilitation, and Aftercare. The strategy outlines goals and challenges for Saudi authorities, and it identifies ways to combat the spread and appeal of extremist ideologies. The strategy is composed of three separate yet interconnected programs aimed at deterring individuals from becoming involved in extremism; promoting the rehabilitation of extremists and individuals who get involved with them; and providing aftercare programs to facilitate reintegration into society after their release from custody. (Boucek, 2008, p. 4)

For the same reasons previously cited, it is possible that a convicted terrorist is released from prison, but rather than leave the country, he may opt to remain in the United States. This subset is the focus of this research.

What could the United States expect by releasing a convicted terrorist into local communities? The public debate in late 2009 surrounding the trial of 9/11 planner Khalid Sheikh Mohammed (KSM) focused not only on the appropriate justice system in which to try him, but also ignited a firestorm of sensitivities associated with having him on American soil. As most would never expect KSM to be freed, let alone reside in

American neighborhoods after murdering nearly 3,000 people, the visibility of his case provides a compelling point of comparison for future discourse on convicted terrorists in America.

For example, one of the plotters convicted of trying to bomb Los Angeles International Airport (also known as the failed Millennium plot) returned to prison for parole violations, after serving time following his plea deal with federal authorities. Specifically, Abdelghani Meskini:

> ...slipped back into a life of crime after completing a six-year sentence. (He) took a job in 2005 as a manager for a suburban Atlanta apartment complex where the U.S. said he participated in drug dealing, prostitution and bank fraud... he violated parole by trying to obtain an assault rifle and lying to authorities. (Hurtado, 2010)

On the surface, there does not appear to be a direct link to terrorism. However, were the methods employed to make money used to support another, as-yet-undetected plot? Were the drug dealing and fraudulent activity somehow financing or contributing to something we do not know about? These activities may not have anything to do with terrorism. However, it is possible, and Americans would not have any idea of knowing about it. Why did Meskini do what he did? What societal factors may have contributed to such behavior? These are just some of the questions we could ask to better understand more about a released terrorist and the ripple effects he may cause.

It is unclear whether Americans have any discernible interest in or reaction to a certain category of terrorist, whether based on the offense, level of success (such as the number of casualties), nationality, or other factors. There may be some cases that trigger a deeply emotional or easily spotted, traceable, and measurable reaction. This will emerge over time. But in order to build public policy effectively, avoid national security problems, serve victim communities respectfully, and implement effective communications, a strategic awareness of the ripple effects that follow a prison sentence is necessary.

C.   LITERATURE REVIEW

A strategic awareness of the post-release period may be approached from a number of angles, and through various literatures and data sets. The literature can be divided into three primary areas to make sense of what ripples are and where they might be felt. Each of these areas can be used to contribute to the scholarship by honing in on the post-prison end of the terrorism continuum.

First, we can look at the "official" narrative, for the kinds of ripples felt by governments and the strains felt by "the system." Second, we can explore ripples felt by the individual terrorist by extending a line from the works of terrorism scholars to the released convict. The extensive research that explains how someone becomes a terrorist may provide an opportunity for reverse engineering an individual and dissuading a convicted terrorist from reentering the business. There is also a nascent literature describing how terrorist groups end, as well as a very limited scholarship about terrorist recidivism and what have been described as "terrorist dropouts." Third, we can explore society's level of awareness on the topic by understanding what factors may be of concern to local communities. The social status of a returning convicted terrorist may range from shame to praise to obscurity, depending upon the social context.

1.   Ripple Effects Are Felt by Government

To date, much of the recent narrative in the United States about captured terrorists has been focused on either (a) those who have not reached trial, such as detainees held at the Guantánamo Bay detention camp, or (b) those who have been prosecuted by the Department of Justice (with rare mention of those who have completed their terms). The fate of the former group continues to evolve, while statistics on the latter group have been proposed as one metric to assess the nation's performance in the global war on terror. Convictions are celebrated, but the post-conviction era remains unknown. Arguably, the complete timeline for a captured—*and eventually released*—terrorist in America has yet to be fully extended.

Capitol Hill provides a look at embryonic perceptions of our population. Preemptive action to address the convicted and released terrorist began to emerge following Faizal Shahzad's attempted bombing of Times Square in May 2010. Shahzad became a naturalized U.S. citizen just 13 months before his targeted attack. Consequently, Senators Lieberman (I–CT) and Brown (R–MA) proposed to strip the nationality of those "joining a foreign terrorist organization or engaging in or supporting hostilities against the United States or its allies" (Terrorist Expatriation Act of 2010, 2010). Such a proposal is significant in itself, as it provides evidence of policymakers continuing to reexamine the suitability of existing judicial mechanisms.

Former U.S. Customs and Border Protection Officer Julia Davis revealed the names of confirmed terrorists who have been tried and convicted in U.S. courts in a 2010 piece for Examiner.com. She notably cites fifteen individuals whose prison term has expired, or is approaching in the near future, and guesses that, "(m)ost Americans are unaware of the fact that convicted terrorists are being released from prisons and might be living next door" (Davis, 2010). Though examining the radicalization issue and the contact between inmates and individuals outside prison walls, Davis does not forecast what we could expect from those convicted terrorists living among us. Awareness is raised, but next steps remain to be seen.

Blogs and other social media artifacts are not normally appropriate sources for academic research. However, they are very useful in detecting and studying emergent issues. For example, a blog posting by retired U.S. Air Force Colonel and Vice President of Academic Research and Development for 5GW Educational Institute Jenni Hesterman voiced concerns about Khalid Ouazzani, a Moroccan native who plead guilty to conspiracy to provide material support to Al Qaeda (Hesterman, 2010). She observed:

> We tend to front load much effort into the capture and conviction of those colluding with al Qaeda, but in actuality, the hard work hasn't yet begun - that of rehabilitation. With so many cases of U.S. citizens fund raising, recruiting and attempting to carry out terrorist operations, we need to *plan now for their eventual return to society*. What will happen to citizens, such as Ouzzani, "Jihad Jane," Zazi and Shahzad (to name just a few) when their prison sentences are over? How will we prepare for their return to society? Should there be an assessment similar to that conducted for sex offenders before we let them walk out of prison and back into our

neighborhoods? We need to do some strategic thinking on the rehabilitation issue now while we have these al Qaeda sympathists (and worse) in custody. (Emphasis added) (Hesterman, 2010)

While Hesterman's focus is on the singular solution of rehabilitation for convicted and released terrorists, the questions she raises have not been part of a broader national discourse.

We can look internationally for examples of convicted and released terrorists and the consequences they have created. The applicability and validity of such an approach is limited because justice and penal systems vary between nations. However, international partners may have a head start on the narrative and be able to define a framework and identify fundamental themes that emerge from this population. According to Lang:

> Punishment reveals what a community values and how it understands legitimate authority. If this is the case, investigating the practices of punishment at the international level can provide some insight into what values and principles the global community holds, as well as which agents it sees as legitimately able to use violence against those who break the law. In other words, how the international community punishes those who commit international crimes can tell us a great deal about the intersection of law, ethics, and politics at the global level. (Lang, 2010)

The post-conviction life of terrorists has generated discussion about sentencing guidelines. Even in cases when life sentences are issued, there have been examples of individuals who are freed from prison. In Sweden, a terrorist sentenced to life in prison for acts in the 1980s had his sentence commuted to 30 years and was permitted to walk away from prison after completing a portion of that term (Swedish Court Reduces Palestinian Terrorist's Life Sentence, 2008).

Another example made headlines in Spain following the release of José Ignacio de Juana Chaos, who "was arrested (in 1987)… and sentenced two years later to more than 3,000 years in prison for killing 25 people in 11 attacks and subsequently to an additional three years for making terrorist threats" (ETA Terrorist Iñaki De Juana Chaos Released from Prison after 21 Years, 2008). Under Spanish law at the time of his conviction, however, he could receive a maximum prison sentence of only 30 years, which "was reduced further because he completed university studies" (ETA Terrorist

Iñaki De Juana Chaos Released from Prison after 21 Years, 2008). Therefore, upon his release from prison in August 2008, José Luis Rodriguez Zapatero, the Spanish Prime Minister, said that he "felt 'scorn' for De Juana Chaos but that 'the law must be respected.'" (ETA Terrorist Iñaki De Juana Chaos Released from Prison after 21 Years, 2008). Three months after his release, Spanish authorities issued a European Arrest Warrant to the Police Service of Northern Ireland on charges that De Juana Chaos praised or supported terrorism in a letter read at a rally (Court Bails ETA Extradition Man, 2008). Spain sought to have him extradited from Ireland, but he jumped bail in March 2010, prior to appealing the ruling (BBC News, 2010).

Those receiving shorter sentences also have caused ripples through their roles in assisting terror cells. Some terrorists convicted of lesser crimes have morphed into dangerous felons. In Indonesia, there are concerns about "several convicts… returning to their old ways" upon their release from prison (Rayda, 2009). For example:

> Bagus Budi Santoso, who was jailed in 2005 for hiding fugitive terrorist Noordin M. Top after the first JW Marriott hotel bombing in 2004, is believed to have played a bigger role in the (2009) bombings of the Marriott and Ritz-Carlton hotels. (Rayda, 2009)

Santoso's original crime was hiding a fugitive terrorist. This lesser crime may have served as the top of a slippery slope for the next iteration of terrorist activity. This case, along with several others, has led the Indonesian Justice and Human Rights Minister to disallow any pardons or remissions for terrorists in the future (Indonesia Says No More Remissions, Pardons for Terror Offenders, 2010).

Like prison sentences, the conditional orders for ex-convicts vary. Some individuals continue to receive constant monitoring, while others have been returned to prison for breaching the terms of their supervised release (Sullivan, 2009). In the United Kingdom, Hamid Elasmar, Zahoor Iqbal, and Mohammed Irfan served fewer than two years in prison for their contribution to a plot aimed at kidnapping and beheading a British Muslim soldier (Goldby, 2009). Despite their release, "the terrorists remain on a Bank of England watchlist restricting their bank accounts, freezing their assets and imposing caps on any financial transactions…. to prevent them using funds to supply overseas terror organisations in the future" (Goldby, 2009). As discussions percolate about homegrown terrorism in the United States, such an example may be reason for concern about individuals who, originally sentenced to short prison sentences, for comparatively minor offenses, could radicalize.

However, what should the limits be on restrictions and surveillance efforts? Political officials have issued statements about the subject, but have offered little, if any, details about proposed actions. Specifically:

- the Australian Attorney-General called for "constant surveillance" to protect the Australian public following the release of convicted terrorist David Hicks (Hicks to be Watched, 2007).

- the British Shadow Home Secretary explained that convicted terrorists are "people who wanted to destroy our way of life, and yet we are leaving them free to roam around this country. It's a crazy state of affairs and we really need to find a way of doing something about it" ('High Risk' Convicted Terrorists Live in Bail Hostels in Britain, 2009).

- a Russian defense minister, at a joint news conference between Russia and the United States in 2005, expressed the need for "close monitoring of people convicted of terrorist offenses after their release from custody" (Convicted Terrorists Should be Watched upon Release, 2005).

Is there an appropriate place or path for an individual to follow following the completion of his prison sentence? Significant ripples were caused when convicted terrorist William McArthur was identified as a worker at London's Heathrow Airport (Rice, 2004). While suitability assessments were not conducted for the contract employee, such an example introduces questions about whether justice is maintained following prison time.

Further along the post-prison narrative are questions about rehabilitation. If releasing a convicted terrorist has ripple effects on both the individual and the community he joins, society may be especially vulnerable when prisons are overcrowded, and prisoners are released early (Johnston, 2008). What responsibility does the state have to assist both the individual and society?

This introduces questions about terrorist recidivism into the discourse. Can a terrorist even be rehabilitated? Should resources be applied to do so? The efficacy of the rehabilitation of ex-convicts has been critiqued, both internationally and in the United States. Evidence of rehabilitation program failures (i.e., 'terrorist alumni' who return to nefarious acts) has been highlighted by legislators as examples of ineffective ways to handle released terrorists (Sherman, 2010).

The International Conference on Terrorist Rehabilitation hosted by the S. Rajaratnam School of International Studies, Nanyang Technological University in Singapore brought presenters from around the world to discuss the issue of terrorist rehabilitation, representing efforts in Iraq, Egypt, Yemen, Saudi Arabia, the United Kingdom, Spain, Uzbekistan, Pakistan, Bangladesh, Singapore, Malaysia, Indonesia, Thailand, and the Philippines (The International Conference on Terrorist Rehabilitation, 2009). No single methodology to deradicalize terrorists was agreed upon, but a multifaceted approach presented many subjects including information operations, religious influences and interpretations, group dynamics, behavior modification, vocational choice, and family counseling as tools to prevent convicted and released terrorists from rejoining their former lifestyles. Some of these subjects may be used in reverse to identify sources for this research, and to determine what ripples are caused by the reentry of a terrorist into American society, and eventually neutralize them.

Successful rehabilitation prevents the ex-convict from returning to a life of terror. In Australia, officials are learning best practices from deradicalization efforts around the world in order to counter the potential effects of a convicted and released terrorist with a weak support system. As stated by Corrective Services deputy commissioner Rod Wise (who attended the conference in Singapore):

> We have now got a number of terrorists who have recently been convicted and sentenced.... We have an obligation to put them back into the community when they are released in such a way that they engage in law-abiding activities. (Higgins, 2009)

Efforts have been focused on "options to introduce deradicalization strategies as part of a broader engagement with the Muslim community to encourage moderate Islam" (Higgins, 2009).

Opportunity for even greater success may come from those 'terrorist alumni' who wish to weaken the institution that got them in trouble in the first place. It is hard to debate that there is no one better to describe the influences in a terrorist's life than a terrorist himself. In Indonesia, police use convicted and released terrorists as "informers or preachers of moderation" to contribute to the international narrative (Forbes & Coorey, 2007). In the United Kingdom, Maajid Nawaz, convicted and sentenced to an Egyptian prison for his membership Hizb ut-Tahrir, co-founded an organization to combat the radicalization of youth, upon his release from prison. Called the Quilliam Foundation, the British- government-funded think tank facilitates dialogue about social issues, and supports "developing a Muslim identity at home in, and with, the West" (About Us, (n.d.). Nawaz speaks to thousands of Muslims and actively participates in the "ideas debate" to discredit the narrative perpetuated by Islamic extremists (Bonin, 2010). Such action provides evidence that ripples can be created for the betterment of society.

The imposition of travel restrictions has also been central to the international narrative when it comes to convicted terrorists. While such an action is designed to minimize the possibility of any ripple effects, there may be newfound complexity within diplomatic circles.

For example, in the case of Parminder Singh Saini, this question has been raised: "is there no reform... or are countries always in retribution mode?" (Singh, 2010). Saini participated in the hijacking of an Air India aircraft in 1984, and upon his conviction and subsequent release from prison, he concealed his identity and moved to Canada to avoid possible death in his native country (Jimenez, 2009). His attempt to reenter society became a challenge because his home country did not want him free within its borders, and his illegally adopted country chose to deport him. "The case pit(ted) the right of the Canadian public to be protected against the international obligation to safeguard people from human rights violations" (Jimenez, 2009). As of January 2010, despite a "15 year peaceful stay in Canada; the Indian authorities have detained him under a preventive detention law, the National Security Act and has lodged him in Tihar prison in Delhi" (Singh, 2010). As the use of preventive detention receives further scrutiny in the United States, the Saini case may introduce questions about how to handle defined terrorists who have completed their prison sentences.

Countries may be continuously in retribution mode, as also seen in the case of French terrorist Willie Brigitte. Just as some nations can ship a convict out, other nations can lock the door to prevent him from coming in. Australia blocked Brigitte from reentering the country for planning terrorist acts there. Where he goes remains to be seen, as some believe it would be "doubtful that he would even be able to leave France as the authorities there are unlikely to issue travel documents to a convicted terrorist" (Neighbour, 2009). Multinational cases present unique challenges for governments. As stated by the Canadian Public Safety Minister:

> Many countries are struggling with the issue of what to do with convicted terrorists who return after their sentences. 'When one of their citizens is convicted in another jurisdiction, serves their time and returns, clearly there could be specific concerns related to that.' (Bell, 2007).

Certainly, there are political ramifications associated with releasing a convicted terrorist. The prospect of Israel releasing Marwan Barghouti, head of the Fatah paramilitary Tanzim organization, has begun to cause ripples that impact the political structure of the region, as Barghouti is among the candidates to lead the Palestinian Authority (Inbari, 2010). Police in the Republic of Maldives needed to use batons and pepper spray to control protesters objecting to the appointment of convicted terrorist Abdullah Shahid as state minister of defense and national security (Maldives Police Disperse Protest against Terrorist as Minister, 2008).

The more visible political case was that of Lockerbie bomber Abdelbaset Ali al-Megrahi, who made headlines when he was released from a Scottish prison by Justice Secretary Kenny MacAskill in August 2009 on "compassionate grounds" following the progression of his terminal prostate cancer (Lockerbie Bomber Freed from Jail, 2009). Al-Megrahi was sentenced to life in prison for the 1988 bombing of Pan Am Flight 103 in December 1988. His celebratory reception by the Libyan people upon his return

26

created an outcry by politicians and victims' organizations questioning the meaning of justice. While al-Megrahi's actions in his last days may not be to execute another attack, his freedom may serve as a greater source of inspiration for those evaluating the consequences of violent activity. This may have been exacerbated by al-Megrahi outliving his expectancy by many months. Waves felt from the release of al-Megrahi also spread into the business world, as "suspicion (was) rife that the release (was) part of a larger trade, oil, and gas understanding between Britain and Libya" (The Monitor's Editorial Board, 2009). In sum, the release of al-Megrahi created ripples that cross-cut multiple facets of the international community.

2.   Ripple Effects Are Felt by the Terrorist and His Organization

The ripples caused by a released terrorist merit further research within the academic literature on terrorism. The current literature is more directed toward how groups endure or how individuals are deradicalized, rather than a detailed discussion on terrorist reentry after prison. A broad look at recent research provided by a sample of experts demonstrates this. First, Bruce Hoffman states:

> The most pressing policy research question so far as terrorism is concerned, accordingly, is… acquiring a better understanding of *how terrorism continues and how some terrorist groups are able to overcome or obviate even the most consequential governmental countermeasures* directed against them. Indeed, it is precisely the elite group of 'survivors'—terrorist groups that have overcome Herculean obstacles, that have surmounted daunting challenges, and that continue despite all odds to persevere (and that al-Qaeda has now joined)—who should concern us greatly. (Emphasis added) (Hoffman, 2009, p. 373)

Convicted terrorists released from prison who have not relinquished their extremist ideology may represent a subset of the "survivors" cited by Hoffman, even though his reference is to groups. Does conviction in a court of law and sentencing to prison qualify as some of the "most consequential governmental countermeasures" he cites? Since examples are beginning to arise that show the release of a convicted terrorist causes some ripple effects, it is fair to assert that a strategy of 'capture, convict, and imprison' is not always a permanent solution, and may require further attention.

Additionally, Hoffman proposes the United States should "re-conceptualize (its national defense strategy) in terms of a global counterinsurgency," to "knit together the equally critical political, economic, diplomatic, and developmental sides inherent to the successful prosecution of counterinsurgency" (Hoffman, 2009, p. 369). He adds that an integrated, "multi-dimensional" approach to include "skills, such as negotiations, psychology, social and cultural anthropology, foreign area studies, complexity theory, and systems management will become increasingly important in the ambiguous and dynamic environment in which irregular adversaries circulate" (Hoffman, 2009, p. 370). This implicitly recognizes that in order to effectively address the impact created by the terrorist organization, an initial awareness of the types of ripple effects created by its members is critical.

Marc Sageman (2009), whose writings pertain to the psychology and individual behaviors of terrorists, has said that focus must be on deradicalization and taking "the glory out of terrorism" (Cronin, Preble, Sageman, & Mack, 2009), and subsequently, reduce the attractiveness of intentionally causing ripples at all. Specifically:

> …the main reason people want to become terrorists… it's to be like the Terminator….they talk about the Terminator, they talk about Rambo… they live in their own fantasy. So you reframe by focusing on victims instead of perpetrators…. You have to challenge their frame that's a war on Islam by focusing more on victims. They're just killers. That's all. (Cronin, Preble, Sageman, & Mack, 2009)

Sageman's perspective reframes the paradigm and introduces a different angle. By better understanding the universe of those affected by terrorism, ripples may be directed toward the released terrorist to minimize his post-prison impact. However, if the glory of being a terrorist still remains—if not increases—following a prison sentence, one could expect the ripples to have adverse consequences.

Audrey Kurth Cronin does not directly address the released terrorist, but she has written extensively about how terrorist groups end. Cronin describes the importance of quelling the ripples created by an imprisoned terrorist: "if a leader is captured and jailed, undermining his credibility and cutting off inflammatory communications are critical to demoralizing his following" (Cronin, 2006, p. 22). However, does opportunity exist to reignite, if not strengthen, that credibility upon release from prison?

Dennis Pluchinsky does recognize the possibility of release from prison, raising concerns in his article, "Global Jihadist Recidivism: A Red Flag." He notes "there are indicators that terrorists, especially global jihadists, have the propensity to return to militancy when released from prison" (Pluchinsky, 2008, pp. 183–184). He also focuses on failure of prison rehabilitation programs as the cause for recidivism, drawing comparisons between criminals and terrorists. By presenting the issue of terrorist recidivism as an independent issue, he recognizes the expanse of the terrorism continuum to reach beyond capture. While he presents the matter as a "global issue and problem for the United States," he acknowledges that this "problem is at its early stages so there is time to address it and develop ways to mitigate it" (Pluchinsky, 2008, p. 189). This research recognizes the need to do just that.

Martha Crenshaw recognizes "the development of terrorism exhibits evolutionary progression, as groups learn from their own experiences and those of others," calling it "highly contingent and reactive" (Crenshaw, 2007, p. 32). However, the lessons of those groups do not appear to have been applied into the post-incident, post-incarceration stage along the continuum. The release of individual terrorists from prison should have its place on that evolutionary progression so more can be learned about the individual, as well as the society and justice system that grapple with these ex-convicts.

Michael Jacobson recognizes the moment of release as a possible "opportunity for people to rethink their support for terrorism or extremist causes" (Jacobson, 2010, p. 1). In *Terrorist Dropouts: Learning from Those Who have Left*, he compiles a set of reasons why individuals quit terrorism. He establishes the fact that there is no single reason, but he states:

> The most common factors include concerns about the organization's direction, goals, or hypocrisy; disappointment with the reality of life in a terrorist or extremist group; and a feeling of being mistreated or undervalued. (Jacobson, 2010, p. 1)

This work may have the closest application to our target of convicted and released terrorists, as it proposes what may be exploited to reduce potential consequences abroad and inside the United States.

3.   Ripple Effects Are Felt by Communities, Not Just Terrorists

Until now, we have mainly spoken about individual terrorists and the direct ripples they have created. However, waves may be created beyond the individual himself. Citizens are still coming to terms with the concept of international terrorists living in America. Steven Emerson's critically acclaimed *American Jihad: The Terrorists Living Among Us* (2002) introduced Islamist extremist groups in the United States, but focused on the unsuspected adversaries instead of those who have been captured, let alone convicted and released from prison.

Limited sources have identified the group of our study as its own phenomenon. Communities that receive convicted terrorists may feel ripples, and can be explored at length through social science frameworks. Works from the fields of criminology, sociology, psychology, and victimology can provide additional lenses for further assessment.

Continued connectivity between the terrorist and the state often exists in some type of supervised release following the completion of the prison sentence. Sutherland, Cressey, and Luckenbill explain that the purpose of both parole and probation is "to adjust the societal response to the circumstances of the offense and the characteristics of the offender" (Sutherland, Cressey & Luckenbill, 1992, p. 556). However, can a societal response be "adjusted" for terrorists released from prison in the same way that criminals are released?

Some evidence suggests terrorists are quickly rejected upon their release from prison, weaving some level of stress into the fabric of the host community. For example, the prison release of Jack Roche, a terrorist convicted of plotting to bomb the Israeli Embassy in Australia, produced headlines ranging from "Release of Roche 'threat' to public" (Release of Roche 'Threat' to Public, 2007) and "Terrorist Freedom Fear," (Terrorist Freedom Fear, 2007) despite other messages conveying "Roche longs for

30

'peaceful life' after serving minimum sentence" (Smiles & Knowles, 2007) and "Terrorist Just Wants a Quiet Life" (Terrorist Just Wants a Quiet Life, 2007). Even when rehabilitation efforts are administered, society may be no less welcoming. As seen in Saudi Arabia:

> Sure (released prisoners) have their freedom back, but they also have a host of challenges to overcome as they try to reintegrate into society. Rejection by society is their main problem. (Khatarish, Al-Qarni, & Al-Jura, 2009)

On the other hand, more homogenous communities may welcome convicted felons with a positive reception, even glorifying them with praise and commitment to the cause. Those who have done prison time may even be elevated as future leaders. As seen in Indonesia:

> In addition, many of their fellow Muslims around them consider those convicted of terrorism offenses to be true and tried "defenders of the faith," "heroes," and they are rewarded with high social status in their communities, circles and groupings." (Ismail, 2010)

Victims groups have deep reasons for struggling with adjusting their response for terrorists released from prison. Reconciliation efforts are challenged frequently by those who lack the ability to forgive. Such a requirement

> …entails that the victim must give up resentment or moral outrage against the offender otherwise reconciliation could not occur… (F)orgiveness in the context of terrorist criminality as a moral imperative is not only incoherent, but a perversion of legality and morality. (Roche, 2010)

Nonetheless, as previously cited, the Saudi rehabilitation program has recognized that justice does not end with the completion of a prison sentence: "For the many prisoners released every day from the Kingdom's prisons, the punishment does not stop when they step out of the prison gate" (Khatarish, Al-Qarni, & Al-Jura, 2009).

So is overall society a victim of terrorism? Simply put, yes, as the act itself spreads beyond the family members of the wounded or deceased. Victims include friends, neighbors, co-workers, associates, emergency management personnel, law enforcement officials, elected representatives, and other figures within the community of the attack. But as Hoffman states, and as previously noted, terrorism is:

31

> ...specifically designed to have *far-reaching* psychological effects *beyond the immediate victim(s)* or object of the terrorist attack.... meant to instill fear within, and thereby intimidate, *a wider "target audience."* (Emphasis added) (Hoffman, 2006, p. 40)

Study of the community beyond the setting of an attack or planned attack is critical to understanding terrorism and its full effects.

To understand and validate societal indicators, such as threat, fear, and rejection requires further research of each ripple. However, while the examples we have provided are revealing, they remain somewhat anecdotal in nature. Formal trends have not been identified, and data are limited. A more expansive literature review within the social sciences will lend insight to how much attention this emergent issue will require in the United States.

III.   METHODOLOGY

For many colleagues, our position will be at best a hypothesis,
to be tested in the years to come; while for many others it is proven fact,
and for others still an article of faith. However colleagues may respond,
our position is not logical; it is phenomenological.

– Glaser & Strauss, 1967, p. 6

A.   INDUCTIVE INQUIRY AND GROUNDED THEORY

Given our exhaustive discussion of what this is not, defining what it is, and presenting a collection of anecdotal evidence and experts' statements connected to the subject of convicted and released terrorists, we set out to locate the pebbles responsible for creating ripple effects on American communities. We are interested because the issue is a national security matter that may present future concerns for governmental, social, political, academic, scientific, and other special interest communities. What we were seeking to discover was a "phenomenological position" as described by Barney Glaser and Anselm Strauss in their 1967 book, *The Discovery of Grounded Theory*.

Glaser and Strauss emphasized the value of using an inductive approach to research that focused on identification of new theory, rather than the more commonly used deductive approach that focused on proving or disproving a theory. The flexibility permitted by grounded theory enables us at the very least to make an attempt at seeing if new theory will emerge from the search for ripple effects created by convicted and released terrorists.

Inductive inquiry serves as the best kind of logic to examine this issue, as it provides an alternative set of rules governing how evidence is handled. Instead of driving toward a solution through deduction, we began with a research question (in this case, "what ripple effects are generated by the release of a convicted terrorist into a host American population?") structured to generate new theory. We were challenged by the fact that our first research question may be rooted in an assumption that is completely

33

false. In other words, we did not even know if ripple effects existed before we began our research and depended upon the emergence of data through the methodology we chose to employ.

This study was originally intended to be exploratory and inductive, observational and grounded, mainly because the United States is early in investigating the paths taken by this adversary upon his release from prison. At this time, requirements for research are less concrete and must be based upon a qualitative understanding of what is taking place and how the environmental conditions are being shaped.

This mirrors the approach taken by homeland security policy makers. Understanding the environment, isolating emergent patterns from categories and properties, learning from those patterns, and developing appropriate actions has served as a framework through which the national enterprise has handled many intergovernmental functions. Since there are many variables in motion—including individual behaviors, the justice system, domestic and foreign influences, and societal pressures, to name a few— we can only gain clarity and discovery by first recognizing the complexity of the issue we are examining. Joshua Ramo has taken notions of complexity and applied them to deep security in *The Age of the Unthinkable*:

> Deep security doesn't answer all of our questions about the future. Indeed, it's predicated on the idea that we don't have all the answers and, in fact, can't even anticipate many of the questions. What it is instead is a way of seeing, of thinking, and of acting that accepts growing complexity and ceaseless newness as givens—and, used properly, our best allies.... *Instead of starting with a view of how we want the world to be and then jamming that view into place, we start more reasonably with a picture of how the world is.* (Emphasis added) (Ramo, 2010, p. 108)

This was the main purpose of our thesis: to develop a preliminary picture of convicted and released terrorists in the United States. Our research recognizes that we are working within the "domain of complexity theory, which studies how patterns emerge through the interaction of many agents" (Kurtz & Snowden, 2003, p. 468).

It would be premature to seek causal relationships and apply deductive logic within this product. A study of convicted and released terrorists a generation from now may warrant a different approach. However, by inquiring about the details surrounding convicted and released terrorists today, we purport that emergent trends will be identified and an initial set of questions will be drawn for multiple groups of society to address in the future. As a U.S. Department of Defense official said in 2007:

> (T)he United States responds to shocks most successfully when it has already recognized and responded to the trends from which they emerge. It is less successful when those trends have gone unidentified or when no effective response to them has been mounted. (Cetron & Davies, 2008, p. ix)

Two central claims were essential to initiate our work on this emerging issue. First, terrorists will continue to be captured, sentenced, imprisoned, and released, especially with the growth of homegrown extremism. Second, ripples will spread as a result of their release into American communities. We expected convicted terrorists to provide us with a trail that we could follow to evaluate these ripples once their prison terms were completed. Yet admittedly, as Christopher Bellavita recognizes, "we can forecast with near certainty some aspects of the future, but their impact on homeland security is unknown" (Bellavita, 2006, p. 6).

Our plan was to examine a small group of individuals and develop a set of rich stories from which we could extract emergent themes and patterns. Different sets of data may produce different outcomes, and the validity of that data may be subject to interpretation if this research were to be repeated. However, as Glaser and Strauss state:

> Since accurate evidence is not so crucial for generating theory, the kind of evidence, as well as the number of cases, is also not so crucial... [The sociologist's] job and his training are to... generate general properties and their categories for general and specific situations and problems. (Glaser & Strauss, 1967, p. 30)

Observable properties may include factors related to who is affected, what activities transpire, and other matters provoked by the release of a convicted terrorist. Our intention was to broaden our collection efforts to strike upon all types of "social phenomena—political, educational, economic, industrial or whatever" (Glaser & Strauss, 1967, p. viii), and find correlations within our universe. We suspected that some metric for ripples would be identified. We thought there might be some level of correlation between the post-prison actions of the terrorist and the societal responses that follow. On one hand, we speculated that some matters could appear and then fade away like a civic rally, while other matters may create complete disruption like new violence and illegal activity. On the other hand, we considered that the size and shape of the ripple may have zero correlation (much less causal connection) to the activity of the terrorist. The terrorist may quietly distance himself from the community, and yet the ripples could still cause huge waves. Regardless of what we would eventually find (or not find), our plan was to describe what we observed of released terrorists, rather than to define causal relationships. As Gerencser et al. (2008) stated:

> Behaviors in a complex system cannot be reliably predicted, but they can be understood. One of the main ways we can employ 'sensing and awareness' is to stop looking for causes and start looking for patterns. (Gerencser et al., 2008, p. 96)

In our search for patterns, we were permitted—*encouraged*, essentially—by grounded theory to stray from existing paths to pursue and identify leads for future trending and analysis. As stated by Glaser and Strauss, "working with borrowed categories is more difficult... focus on the *emergence* of categories solves the problems of fit, relevance, forcing, and richness" (Glaser & Strauss, 1967, p. 37). We planned to avoid bias through collection and analysis. Parameters were to be set once data were coded and collated. While certain 'buckets' may already exist, we recognized how critical it is to avoid such labeling until all material had been explored. Such a concern of the researcher is described below:

> He then becomes caught up in the delights of generating theory, and so compares everything comparable; but the next he finds theory development severely limited by lack of enough theoretically relevant data, because he has used a preplanned set of groups for collecting his information. (Glaser & Strauss, 1967, p. 51)

Therefore, *any* data point obtained might be seen as theoretically relevant, and could present us with a sign of visible stress created by the release of a convicted terrorist in America. The research was intended to be based on a "logic of ongoing inclusion of groups," instead of verification, since the "effort of purification is made for a result impossible to achieve, since one really never knows what has and has not been held constant" (Glaser & Strauss, 1967, p. 50). Outlying issues were subsequently quite welcomed in this research, as these examples can allow us to recognize the breadth of the environment we are trying to understand and substantiate whether or not a phenomenon is on the horizon.

B.   ANTICIPATED PHENOMENA

The actual symptoms, behaviors, markers, or indicators of a terrorist in the community, whether it is in the form of stress, discomfort, or new activity remain to be seen. Yet it is obvious that we can see a spectrum of potential outcomes that may accompany the release of a convicted terrorist from prison, even though categories were undefined at the start of our research. Given the time constraints of the project, we created some structure and shape for this inquiry. In pure grounded theory or a longitudinal study, this is not necessary; but by taking such action we made our work manageable and provided a sense-making framework to articulate what we anticipated so we knew what to look for and where to look.

Clearly, our findings are not conclusive, but they can be used as a starting point for others to build upon. In a report issued by the National Consortium for the Study of Terrorism and Responses to Terrorism (START) based at the University of Maryland, a data and methods task force stated, "almost no research in terrorism has explored either archival data or community-level data related to radicalization" (Human Factors/Behavioral Sciences Division, 2010, p. 15). Our intended search for community-level data was broad, to include places where outcomes might lie within and beyond those centered on the convicted terrorist.

Law enforcement officials and correctional institutions are not the only entities affected by this development. The release of a terrorist may have effects upon his or her new community, former communities, victims, and their families. Such a scenario may appear to be unfathomable to the general population because many have not allowed themselves to believe that it is even possible. Yet it is quite fathomable. The reality of convicted terrorists leaving American prisons remains either unidentified or ignored by the general public.

It could be argued that his former community—the place he deceived, or targeted—will react as the victim literature predicts, with continuous struggle over matters of reconciliation and forgiveness predominating the discourse. However, in addition to the neighborhoods of victims or the original hometown of the ex-convict, impact may also be felt where he resides after prison. It is possible that feelings may run as strongly as those held by the direct victim community. Our intention was not to validate any of the listed possibilities for the individual terrorist or the community, but simply to describe them based on what we identified.

Let us start at the extreme end of the spectrum. It is possible that the release of a convicted terrorist is a major event. The most ripples would be evident if the individual reengaged in terrorist activity, meeting the definition of a true recidivist. Worst-case scenario, he would be at the center of a new plot either as a planner or an operative. He might recruit new members. The effectiveness of the corrections system would be called into question. Considerations for rehabilitation and deprogramming efforts would be nullified. Sentencing guidelines and suggestions for amnesty or commutations might be challenged. Military courts might be advocated over civilian courts. Law enforcement and other facets of the justice system might play an active role in his post-prison life.

Socially speaking, a convicted terrorist in the community could also cause public outrage and initiate calls for banishment for fears of contagion. Even though the individual might never have harmed someone in his new neighborhood—and perhaps never killed anyone at all—the general public could feel as affected as the original targets. "NIMBY" (not in my backyard) could reach a fevered pitch, with public protests, spikes in criminal activity and medical services, heightened religious discourse or confrontations, publication of editorials screaming for stronger detainment policies, and engagement by political officials and special interest groups.

Moving away from the inflammatory side of the spectrum, there could be other serious ripple effects: A forced relationship caused between the convicted terrorist and the state could drive the individual to serve an active role either for or against his former cause. The frame may vary, as individuals tend to be both victims and beneficiaries of their own experiences. Prison could reform an individual, and lead him down the path of educator, so he can advise others away from a terror-focused path. However, imprisonment could also further radicalize someone.

Regardless of the convicted terrorist's actions, any knowledge of his release could create ripples of heightened public fear or suspicion. Citizens might maintain confidence in the judicial system and recognize that the convict "did his time," but still demonize or fear him. Notification of a convicted terrorist in the neighborhood could trigger calls for increased surveillance and monitoring. Shaming techniques could be utilized by special interest groups or politicians seeking to mitigate repeat behavior or increased radicalization in the community, in ways similar to those used against sexual and child predators.

As for the other side of the spectrum, the release of a convicted terrorist might very well be a non-event, especially if he moves into a community that did not suffer directly from his crimes. An individual locked up for 20 months or time served may not be perceived as alarming as an individual locked up for 20 years (on the logic that their crimes must have been much less severe), especially if they mind their business and keep reasonable distance.

It is also possible that the press may never have heard of the terrorist before his conviction, and may have no interest in him after his release. He might fade into obscurity, distant from his former life, both literally and symbolically. Our broad social respect for privacy could explain why a community would never notice if a terrorist were to move into the neighborhood. In either case, no subsequent ripples would be visible to the outside eye. The only lasting record of the person as a terrorist would rest in the files of a probation officer, the National Crime Information Center database, and the memory of the individual himself.

C.   DISCLAIMER IN USING GROUNDED THEORY

While we did not have expectations for what would be identified or how such information could be measured or defined, this research was designed to understand the environmental conditions and emergent themes stemming from the reemergence of a convicted terrorist in American society.

Such an assumption is actually counter to grounded theory, because it, as lawyers say, "assumes facts not in evidence." The project was in fact preliminarily called "Ripples of the convicted and released terrorist," on the assumption that ripples would exist. In other words, one might argue that we violated the conventions of grounded theory from the beginning. Be that as it may, below are the steps we took to identify new theory.

D.   CASE SELECTION

A first step was to identify those who qualified as convicted and released terrorists. Interestingly, we were unable to find any source that analytically addressed such a group. However, there were data on the larger convicted terrorist population from which we could begin.

The size of the sample pool was not critical for our purposes. Nevertheless, as a point of reference, the National Security Division of DOJ released a report to the Senate Judiciary Committee in March 2010 showing the convictions of 403 people for planning or committing international terrorist attacks since 9/11 (Introduction to National Security Division Statistics on Unsealed International Terrorism and Terrorism-Related Convictions, 2010).

Prior to release of the DOJ report, the non-profit organization Human Rights First (HRF) published *In Pursuit of Justice: Prosecuting Terrorism Cases in the Federal Courts* in 2008, and updated its dataset in 2009. These studies used a narrower definition of "terrorism cases to encompass prosecutions that are related to Islamist extremist terrorist organizations, such as al Qaeda or individuals and organizations that are ideologically or organizationally linked to such groups" (Zabel & Benjamin, 2009).

Much of the scholarly literature and government documentation relies on similar definitions or demographic limiters: our research, too, therefore, focused on defendants with a nexus to Islamist terrorism. As the HRF report cites:

> In this Paper we use terms, such as "jihad" and "Islamic"—terms that are frequently used by terrorist groups themselves and employed by others who have analyzed terrorism and terrorist organizations. Throughout the Paper we have qualified these terms (e.g., "self-described jihadist") to make clear that they are intended to be descriptive. In no way are any of these words intended to imply that what self-described jihadists or Islamist extremist groups say or do is consistent with Islam. (Zabel & Benjamin, 2009, p. 143)

The same disclosure applies here: our starting point was the dataset of 171 terrorism convictions provided by—and thus, the definitions and demographic profiles used by—HRF (Zabel & Benjamin, 2009, p. 5). Of the 171 defendants cited, sentence terms varied based on the following distribution, in terms of years, as seen in Figure 3.

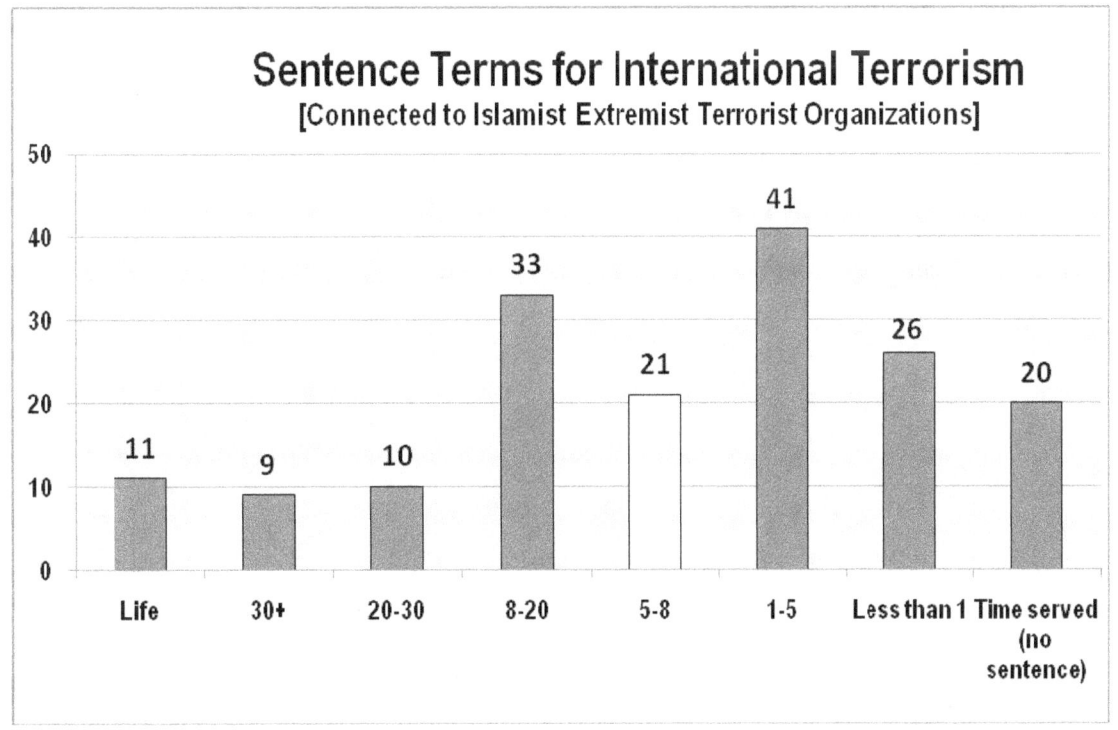

Figure 3. Sentence Terms for International Terrorism (From: Zabel & Benjamin, 2009)

The data reflected here clearly depict the reality of finite sentencing for those convicted of terrorism-related crimes. Only eleven of the 171 convictions resulted in a life sentence. In the United Kingdom, by comparison, life sentences were handed out to "23 of the 230 people convicted on terrorism or terrorism-related offences as a result of the first wave of jihadist attacks against Britain since 9/11" (A. Travis, 2010).

Our area of initial interest for research was the 21 defendants who received sentences of 5-8 years. We looked at those with the longest sentences who have since been released, assuming that this was the subset of released people who were convicted for the worst crimes. While this logic does have its flaws (as it does not account for variables, such as deals for information, or the advantages of superior legal representation), at a minimum, it set us on a path to begin the study. Of the 21 defendants, the Federal Bureau of Prisons revealed that as of May 2010, fifteen had been released, one was still imprisoned, and the status of five people was unknown (BOP: Inmate Locator Main Page, n.d.).

E.   INTENDED DIRECTION

1.   Data Collection

Our next challenge was to identify the locations of the individuals following their release. We decided to limit the scope and tools of this research to open sources rather than classified, since this would approximate the investigative avenues and information sources available to the general public.

In addition to using investigative tactics through internet research of mainstream media, social networking sites, and other public records, queries were conducted by leveraging databases, such as Lexis-Nexus and ProQuest that integrate multiple media channels, as well as scholarly publications. Obtaining court documents also provided us with a starting point to collect information, as case dockets report the actions leading up to the beginning of our place on the terrorism continuum—when a convicted terrorist is released from prison. Dates were to be used as reference points for capturing statements by public officials, press releases, editorials, and local police reports.

Such background information about our selected individuals was then to be used to steer further research to gain insight about the released terrorist, both historically and within the current context. We considered interviewing local law enforcement officials, as well as citizen preparedness or active community groups, to gauge the breadth of the ripples in the areas where these individuals now reside.

This would in principle have provided us with an understanding of where citizens rank convicted terrorists among other types of criminals, such as arsonists, burglars, and sex offenders. Does the public believe convicted terrorists who have done prison time can repay their debt to society? Would people feel at risk if they knew that one of them had joined their community after completing a prison sentence? What might such knowledge cause citizens to do? Would they expect government to do something about it, and what would "it" be?

2.   Comparative Analysis

Our intention was to obtain a variety of leads that furnished enough data on a handful of individuals to direct us in a methodical manner to better understand our subject. These data were to be used to develop a sample of robust case studies for comparative analysis from which we could propose categories and properties. Comparing one member of our dataset with another allows for similarities and differences to emerge. According to Glaser and Strauss:

> (E)lements of theory that are generated by a comparative analysis are, first, conceptual categories and their conceptual properties; and second, hypotheses or generalized relations among the categories and their properties... A category stands by itself as a conceptual element of the theory. A property, in turn, is a conceptual aspect or element of a category... Categories and properties 'have a life apart from the evidence that gave rise to them.' (Glaser & Strauss, 1967, pp. 35–36)

Identifying "categories and their properties" and how they relate to the network of stakeholders would provide a baseline for additional validation and use of comparative tools in future research with a more statistically significant population.

F. LIMITATIONS

We anticipated the research to be challenged by limited opportunities to assess ripples within an American context. First, it seemed reasonable to expect that the release of a non-citizen would result in immediate deportation following completion of a prison sentence. Second, because our dataset (fortunately) did not include those who have directly killed American citizens, we expected the ripples to be fewer and smaller than otherwise. Our population was comprised of those convicted of crimes other than murder, sentenced to terms based on indirect crimes with lesser punitive consequences. In other words, we cannot focus on the "worst of the worst," who will be locked up indefinitely or killed in the commission of his crime. Third, this research would be more fruitful if we had a larger dataset to work with. Fourth, working without restricted or limited sources limited our ability to fully investigate our subject. In-house resources in a classified or an FOUO (for official use only) environment would certainly have expedited the location of those in our dataset, as opposed to conducting a Freedom of Information Act (FOIA) inquiry. Brannan, Esler, and Strindberg (2001) acknowledge the variance between public and in-house analysis:

> Threat analyses based on secondary or tertiary sources and tailored to the perspective of the commissioning agency are just as easily produced using in-house analysts, often with a far better access to sources. (Brannan, Esler, & Strindberg, 2001, p. 20)

It might have been be helpful to know if, for example, an individual who left the U.S. upon completion of his sentence did so voluntarily or involuntarily. Such information, however, is not for public consumption unless government agencies release it. Regardless of what we do not have, our intention was to work with the findings we generated to inform the general public on whether or not a phenomenon exists that is worthy of continued exploration.

IV. THE SYSTEM

Process without passion is bureaucracy.

- Gerencser et al., 2008, p. 214

A. ASSEMBLY LINE

Research revealed an extensive collection of historical material about the indictments, arrests, convictions, and sentencing of terrorists in the United States. However, the stories stopped here. While release dates for 21 convicted terrorists could be researched through the Federal Bureau of Prisons (BOP) website, we could not find information about the pending release or post-incarceration status of the any of the listed names. As a result, we were unable to develop a comparative analysis between subjects.

Thus, we turned to an inquiry of the administrative process when a prison sentence ends and the prospect of freedom emerges. Learning about those parties who are administratively responsible for the convicted terrorist ultimately may be used to identify the location of convicted and released terrorists.

Consequently, we modified the course of our methodology and redirected our study from the ripples we anticipated that the community would feel, toward the pebble: the convicted terrorist. The end of the prison term and the transition between incarceration and freedom is what Travis recognizes as the

> …critical step in the assembly line [that] receives the least attention in the world of criminal justice practice. Yet this is where hundreds of thousands of Americans each year make difficult and dangerous transitions in ways that affect their sense of identity, their relationships with family and community, and their chances of successful reintegration into society. (J. Travis, 2006, p. 333)

Exploring the multiple disciplines that interact with our target of study helped us better understand those stakeholders with connected responsibilities in the homeland security network, and enabled us to assess the extent to which this niche population received special attention. It also introduced the opportunity to support or challenge the systemic design established for the convicted terrorist as he progresses from incarceration to freedom. Moreover, we were able to extract discussion points that contribute to the ongoing dialogue about the differences between terrorists and criminals, introducing a policy discussion for the next phase of the terrorism continuum.

Informal background discussions with government officials were essential to gaining a perspective of what a convicted terrorist may experience. Law enforcement officers, prison officials, probation officers, attorneys, and community outreach specialists were some of the representatives who provided a baseline of knowledge that was used to develop a descriptive understanding of the path of the convicted terrorist.

In addition to learning about the core functions within each discipline, we discussed what considerations, if any, have been made for the terrorist reentering society in the United States. Did our colleagues know if the person was still in the United States? Would they know how to obtain personal contacts of the individual? Where did they think his impact would be felt today?

1. Federal Law and Order

Law enforcement is the first discipline to have contact with the convicted terrorist. The Federal Bureau of Investigation (FBI) has jurisdiction over violations of more than 200 categories of federal law, including counterterrorism, both international and domestic (FBI—What We Investigate, n.d.). Special agents of the Bureau may be joined by multiple agencies including the Departments of the Treasury and Commerce, Bureau of Alcohol, Tobacco and Firearms (ATF), Drug Enforcement Administration (DEA), and Immigration and Customs Enforcement (ICE) to investigate an array of terrorism-related activities. Joint Terrorism Task Forces (JTTFs) provide the forum for such multijurisdictional, collaborative terrorism investigations.

Upon arrest by a federal agent (or deputized state or local agent), prisoners are held in the custody of the U.S. Marshal. Following prosecution by the U.S. Attorney's Office and conviction in a federal court, defendants are remanded to the custody of the Attorney General, which is delegated to the Federal Bureau of Prisons (BOP). There is little reason for the investigating agent, the U.S. Marshal, or the U.S. Attorney to remain engaged with the defendant following the sentence.

2. Federal Bureau of Prisons

Correctional facilities have contact with and jurisdiction over the convict during his incarceration. Information collected by BOP is used to examine what other entities and disciplines interact with a convict, and to identify his post-incarceration whereabouts.[5] For each inmate, BOP forwards a Supervision Release Plan to a probation office.[6] Probation offices are responsible for coordinating supervision of "persons released to the community by the courts and paroling authorities" (Probation and Pretrial Services—Mission). The Supervision Release Plan requires a released convict to report to his probation officer within 72 hours of release, provide residential and employment intentions, and adhere to certain requirements (Supervision Release Form) that give officers tools for supervision, such as warrantless search procedures, alcohol and drug restrictions, and Internet activity monitoring. It is possible for a district probation office to refuse a plan that does not account for counseling services, employment opportunities, and family or personal contacts.

BOP also generates a Notice of Release and Arrival form, which collects the address of proposed residence and the jurisdiction for supervision of prisoner upon his release (Notice of Release and Arrival Form, n.d.).

---

[5] We do not focus on the impact of the correctional system on a convicted terrorist, as a separate, extensive sect of literature has been written about how prison may serve as a place for radicalization and deradicalization of inmates. This research is interested only in how a convict transitions into society upon release from prison.

[6] The Sentencing Reform Act of 1987 replaced federal *parole* with *supervised release*. U.S. Probation Officers supervise those offenders placed on *supervised release* and/or *probation*. The terms and conditions of each are the same, except that *supervised release* is the term used for the supervision following a term of imprisonment, while *probation* is issued in place of imprisonment.

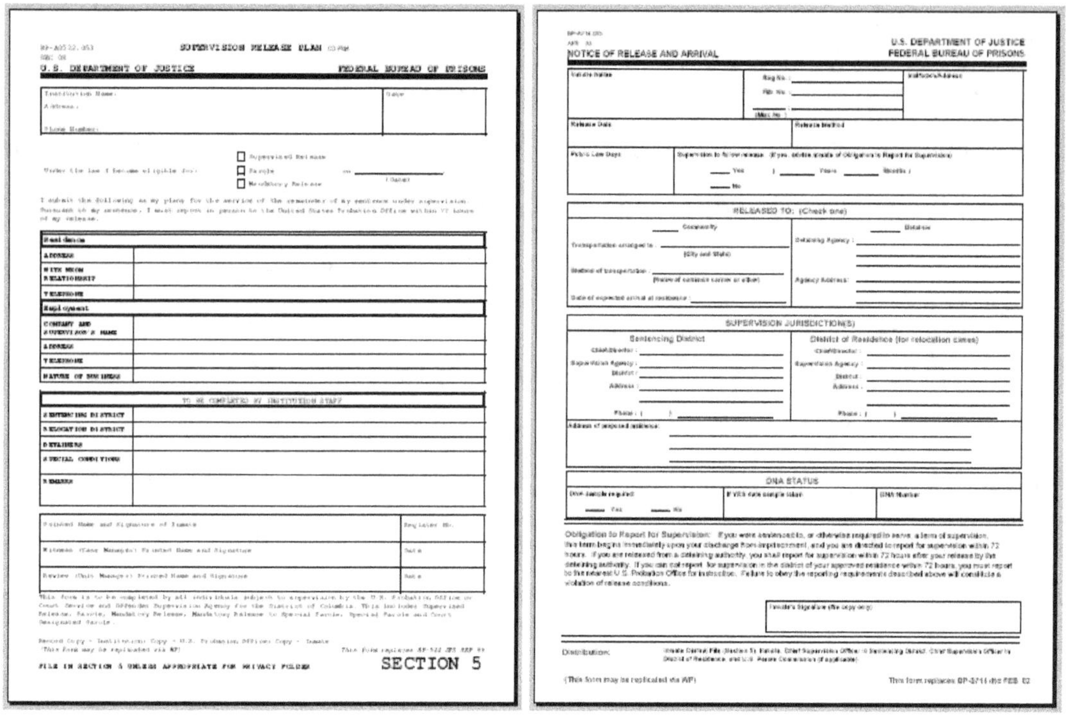
SUPERVISION RELEASE PLAN

U.S. DEPARTMENT OF JUSTICE

FEDERAL BUREAU OF PRISONS

SECTION 5

NOTICE OF RELEASE AND ARRIVAL

U.S. DEPARTMENT OF JUSTICE

FEDERAL BUREAU OF PRISONS

RELEASED TO: (Check one)

SUPERVISION JURISDICTION(S)

DNA STATUS

Figure 4. Supervision Release Plan and Notice of Release and Arrival forms

We initiated a Freedom of Information Act (FOIA) request to BOP for a copy of: (1) the Supervision Release Plan; (2) the Notice of Release and Arrival; and (3) contact information of the probation officer for each of the 21 names in our dataset. Our objective was to identify the post-prison location of convicted and released terrorists, in order to determine where (and if) direct ripple effects existed. As previously mentioned, there are not many resources that could be used to know if a convicted terrorist lived nearby, unless the individual were to call attention to himself.

At the conclusion of a search for records from the National Archives, the BOP FOIA Office returned 37 pages of material, but the content was so redacted that not one page listed the name of one inmate, due to privacy exemptions. The five-month inquiry furnished 17 Supervision Release Plans, 18 Notice of Release & Arrival plans, and two Release of Immigration Detained with Supervision to Follow forms. Even though the introductory letter seen in Figure 5 stated, "no records have been withheld in their entirety," the documents retained only the headers and footers designating what materials were pulled, and the district where the individual was sentenced.

Re: Information Request No. 2010-10152

Dear Mr. Brown:

On November 29, 2010, the Bureau of Prisons (BOP) received you payment in the amount of $40.00, associated with the above referenced request.

As previously advised, thirty-seven (37) pages of records were located responsive to your request. After careful review we have determined that these pages can be released with certain information redacted. No records have been withheld in their entirety. These releasable records are enclosed.

Pursuant to the Freedom of Information Act, 5 U.S.C. 552(b)(2)-(7), records are exempt in part from disclosure to you under the following exemptions:

(b)(6) -personnel and medical files and similar files the disclosure of which would constitute a clearly unwarranted invasion of personal privacy
(b)(7)(C) - constitutes an unwarranted invasion of personal privacy

Figure 5. DOJ/BOP FOIA Response

From the limited material we did receive, we can deduce some analytical points, notwithstanding the speculative nature upon which these are based. First, by not even listing the names of the individuals in these respective sentencing districts, and requiring us to play a match game between defendant names and sentencing districts, it is evident that providing the locations of released convicts is beyond the interests or powers of the FOIA office. Second, we may assume that 16 of the 18 ex-convicts identified by the FOIA office remained in their sentencing districts upon release, since two Notice of Release & Arrival plans had listings for "District of Residence for relocation cases." Third, we may speculate that since two individuals were released to ICE as noted by the "Release of Immigration Detained with Supervision to Follow" forms, that 16 remained in the United States after their release. Fourth, the completely redacted Supervision Release Plans demonstrate that public notification of the release of a convicted terrorist (or criminal for that matter) is not a priority, responsibility, or requirement of the U.S. government, nor is the general public seen as a stakeholder in the process of release.

The BOP FOIA Office did provide Public Information Inmate Data forms for many convicts listed in our request (Federal Bureau of Prisons, 2010). These forms summarize court actions and list sentencing and supervision terms for those who have spent time in federal prison. Also included are the phone numbers of the prison where the convict was detained, but proposed post-prison residence information is not provided. A complete list is provided in Table 3. As of August 2010, summarized findings for the 21 individuals in our sample are listed below:

- 18 were ordered terms of supervised release, between two and five years; of the 18 individuals:

    - Prison and supervised release had ended for two individuals.

    - Prison and supervised release were scheduled to end for:

        - twelve individuals by the end of 2012,
        - one individual in 2013, and
        - one individual in 2015.

    - Two were not scheduled for prison release until 2012 and 2018.

- Three were not identified by BOP.

Table 3. Convicted and Released (or soon to be released) Terrorists (After: Zabel & Benjamin, 2009 (Names); BOP: Inmate locator main page, n.d.) (Conviction and Release Data)

Defendant	Name	Conviction	Release
1	Baz Mohammad	Conspiracy to import heroin	01/07/12
2	Muhammad Ibrahim Bilal	("Portland Seven") Conspiracy to contribute services to the Taliban and conspiracy to possess firearms	09/22/09
3	Shafal Mosed	("Lackawanna Six") Providing material support or resources to designated FTO	09/01/09
4	Yasein Taher	("Lackawanna Six") [Not identified]	
5	Bayan Elashi	Conspiracy to violate the export admin regulations & the Libyan sanctions regulation; Libyan export violations; money laundering; dealing in property of a specifically designated terrorist & aiding & abetting	01/22/09
6	Faysal Galab	("Lackawanna Six") ...contribution of funds, goods, services to and for benefit of specially designated terrorists	10/17/08
7	Maher "Mike" Hawash	("Portland Seven") Conspiracy to contribute services to the Taliban	04/14/09
8	Youssef Hmimssa	Conspiracy to commit offense or to defraud the United States; fraud and misuse of visas, permits, and other documents	05/25/07
9	Basman Elashi	Conspiracy to violate the export admin regulations & the Libyan sanctions regulation; Libyan export violations; false statement; Syrian export violation; money laundering	10/08/08
10	Ahmad Nesar Bashash	Conspiracy to distribute heroin	06/02/08
11	Bashir Ahmad Rahmany	Conspiracy to import heroin; conspiracy to distribute and possess with intent to distribute heroin	08/25/10
12	Elias Akhdar	Conspiracy to violate the Racketeer Influenced & Corruptions Act (RICO)	03/05/08
13	Javed Iqbal	[Not identified]	
14	Cedric Carpenter	Conspiracy to provide material support & resources to a foreign terrorist organization felon in possession of a firearm	09/05/09
15	Shah Mohmood	[Not identified]	
16	Hazim Elashi	Conspiracy to violate the export admin regulations & the Libyan sanctions regulation; Libyan export violations; false statement; Syrian export violation; money laundering, conspiracy to file false shipper's export declaration forms	04/26/07
17	James Elshafay	("Herald Square Plot") Conspiracy to damage & destroy by means of explosive, real property used in interstate commerce	01/28/09
18	Khalid Awan	Conspiracy to provide & providing material support to terrorists; money laundering	05/15/18
19	Naji Abi Khalil	Conspiracy to launder money; attempting to provide material support to a terrorist organization; attempting to contribute goods to a specially designated terrorist; conspiracy against the U.S.	10/17/08
20	Numan Maflahi	Making false statement to a federal officer	11/06/08
21	Ronald Grecula	Attempting to provide support & resources to a designated foreign terrorist organization	09/25/09

Remarkably, one individual was listed for release in August 2010; but according to an official at the prison where he was detained, he was still listed as a current inmate. While tangential, this discovery introduces a whole conversation about reconciliation between databases and information sharing issues that may exist both within and between disciplines. If we are to identify the ripple effects created by released prisoners, accurate systems must be in place to identify their locations, especially while they are in custody.

Also notable is the three individuals who were not identified as having records with BOP. While their names appeared in federal indictments, no reasons were given for their absence. We may only speculate that these three convicts' names were either spelled incorrectly, prison time was never served, or new identity protections were put in place.

3.   Federal Probation and Pretrial Services System

The next stop for a convict is with his probation officer. The Federal Probation and Pretrial Services System is part of the judicial branch of the U.S. government. Its officers are "the 'eyes and ears' of the federal courts," work for a judge, and "investigate and supervise persons charged with or convicted of federal crimes" (Probation and Pretrial Services—Mission). Federal probation officers work with the executive branch of government through BOP, U.S. attorneys, and U.S. marshals to administer their caseloads. Their national database is used to ensure convicts do not fall through the cracks upon leaving prison.

Supervision Release Plan and Notice of Release and Arrival forms are forwarded by BOP to district probation offices. The documentation becomes part of the probationer's case file, and remains property of the court. Information from these forms may be released to BOP, the U.S. Sentencing Commission, and law enforcement. Not all prisoners provide residential information, and there are examples of individuals who walk out of prison without reporting to a probation officer within the 72-hour requirement. Those who do provide information may move frequently, making ongoing supervision a challenge. Many do not even have conditions upon release. In fact, Travis states, "about one-fifth of the more than 630,000 prisoners released annually from America's state and federal prisons are released unconditionally" (J. Travis, 2006, p. xxii).

Individuals who receive probation can be tracked through a handful of channels. Probation officers begin supervision by reviewing the federal criminal judgment. These judgments include standard conditions of supervised release, which require individuals to submit a truthful written report each month indicating where they live and work. Under certain conditions, probation officers can visit home at any time, seize contraband in plain view, order instructions, and conduct warrantless searches for reasonable suspicion of violations. A judgment that requires periodic drug testing serves as a valuable tracking tool; although, it does not help the public know where the convicts are located. In addition to the forms provided by BOP and federal criminal judgments, probation officers can also obtain federal court orders to review contents of email threads through Internet service providers or bank records through financial institutions, without probable cause under a warrantless search condition.

Ripple effects may be felt in communities during the period of supervision and the period that follows:

> In considering the challenges of prisoner reentry, we must focus squarely on the criminal sanctions that apply after the prison gates close and after the period of supervision is over. There is little research on the impact of these sanctions; however, from the perspective of the returning prisoners, they pose steep hurdles on the road to reintegration. Long after the prison time has been served and parole has been completed, the ex-felon is frequently reminded that his debt has not been paid as society continues to extract a price for violating its laws. (J. Travis, 2006, pp. 63–64)

Probation officers may observe ripple effects in local communities when supervision is administered. When a convict is released from custody, the visits of a probation officer and occasional probing of neighbors for residential verification may cause some waves. Employers notified of an employee's prior conviction may further stigmatize the individual and may trigger ripples beyond the period of supervision.

Unfortunately, we were unable to contact a probation officer of a convicted terrorist as part of our research. The judicial branch is exempt from FOIA requests (FOIA Guide, 2004), leaving us to rely on BOP in the executive branch to obtain information.

However, a background discussion with an official within the Administrative Office of the U.S. Courts revealed that there were no notable post-9/11 policies issued by the Judicial Conference of the United States that may have altered the way supervised release is applied for those convicted of terrorism-related crimes. Legislatively, to the contrary, one of the highest-profile laws in the United States since 9/11 called to amend Section 3583 of Title 18 of the U.S. Code *to specifically address post-release supervision of terrorists*. Section 812(j) of The Uniting and Strengthening America by Providing Appropriate Tools Required to Intercept and Obstruct Terrorism Act of 2001 (better known as the USA PATRIOT Act), states:

> **Supervised release terms for terrorism predicates-** Notwithstanding subsection (b), the authorized term of supervised release for any offense listed in section 2332b(g)(5)(B), the commission of which resulted in, or created a foreseeable risk of, death or serious bodily injury to another person, is any term of years or life. (Uniting and Strengthening America by Providing Appropriate Tools Required to Intercept and Obstruct Terrorism (USA PATRIOT ACT) Act of 2001, 2001)

The offenses cited in the listed section are a full set of terrorism-related crimes, including the ones committed by those in our dataset (Acts of Terrorism Transcending National Boundaries). Yet interestingly, our data showed that no one was ordered more than five years of supervised release, despite the available legal option of life supervision.

At this point in our research, we began to deviate from our intended direction. While the following sections provide additional sources and disciplines that may contain the data we are searching for, the likelihood of obtaining such information in the public realm is quite low. One reason is confidentiality. Currently, the government and the individual's legal representation have no incentive to divulge the location of an individual to the general public. Whether confidentiality is maintained for individual protection or personal privacy, obtaining information on a U.S. citizen—especially one who has been the target of investigation—has its limitations. Another reason is low priority. Current agency missions have not seen convicted and released terrorists as a population of concern to date. Infrastructure may exist to inform and educate the community about the release of such individuals, but resources are currently not used in this manner.

4. Witness Protection, Deportation

Should an individual require supervision and witness protection as provided by the U.S. Marshals Service, a witness security officer within the probation office is notified to facilitate transition between the courts and the general public.[7]

Should deportation be ordered by the judiciary, the individual is released to the Office of Detention and Removal (DRO) of ICE after serving a criminal sentence. Probation officers communicate with ICE to confirm deportation status and to request notifications of future border crossings.

However, there may be time after the completion of prison but prior to deportation before a host country agrees to receive the convict. Some nations resist or deny repatriation once someone has been found guilty of terrorist activity. Until a destination can be identified, and without grounds for detainment, an individual is permitted to enter American communities, so long as he reports his status to ICE and/or his probation officer. This scenario may introduce the opportunity for significant ripple effects, if a local neighborhood were to become aware of the situation.

Formal searches for evidence of immigration court orders were unsuccessful. However, informal contact with government officials allowed us to speculate about the possible whereabouts of two convicted terrorists awaiting deportation. This was as close as we got to finding one of the subjects of our study. However, online searches in the surrounding areas were unable to confirm their residence, requiring us to rely only on insider information to proceed, which was beyond the tools we allowed for this research.

5. Local Law and Order

Once a convict begins reentry, supervision may continue at the local level of government after the federal authorities' period of supervised release ends. The Violent Crime Control and Law Enforcement Act of 1994 requires probation officers to provide notice of release, criminal history, change of residence, and restrictions or conditions of

---

[7] We did not investigate the effectiveness of witness protection programs to track members of our dataset. We assumed that we would not be able to identify ripple effects from a population managed in a covert environment.

release "to the chief law enforcement officer of the State and of the local jurisdiction in which the prisoner will reside," for crimes of drug trafficking, violence, and sex offense (Violent Crime Control and Law Enforcement Act of 1994, p. 39; 18 U.S.C. § 4042 (b) and (c)). Terrorism or material support of terrorism, however, is not specifically listed. Localities may also require probation officers to notify jurisdictions of the release of other types of convicts, such as for those convicted on charges related to firearms. Sex offenders are the only type of criminals required to publicly register upon joining a new community, and electronic monitoring is used as a tracking tool.[8]

The designation of "violent crime" introduces a noteworthy point for discussing whom we have defined as terrorists. Travis says, "A strong public safety argument can be made that, at a minimum, our sentencing system should require postrelease supervision for all violent prisoners" (J. Travis, 2006, p. 55) Can conspiracy to aid the Taliban and providing material support to al Qaeda qualify in this category of "violent," even if no one is directly injured or killed?

Our description of terrorism-related crimes expands beyond those "worst of the worst" individuals who have been convicted of murder. Should supervision requirements be stricter for those who are associated with crimes related to issues of national security, or in the minds of some, treason? Might it be rational to question if a dangerous threat can be posed by those convicted of non-violent, but still terrorism-related, crimes carrying lesser punitive consequences? And if so, should local law enforcement and the general public, be informed of the re-entry of a terrorist in American communities? Would a neighborhood benefit by receiving communications and heightened awareness about its residents? Or would this ignite a counterproductive firestorm of activity within society? Direct victims of crimes are notified by probation offices of the release of a criminal; but do participants in terrorism-related activity require more expansive notifications to the public, because such acts affect national security? What should American communities know?

---

[8] Some localities require convicted felons to register with the police department. However, information is not for public record, and is kept for law enforcement purposes. For example, see Las Vegas Metropolitan Police Department, Crime, Criminal Registration: http://www.lvmpd.com/crime/convict_sexoffender_registration.html.

6.   Community Outreach

This brings us to another component of the system that could help us identify the location of a convicted terrorist. Community outreach is a function not directly related to the assembly line we described, but provides a role that is leveraged by public agencies to strengthen communication between the government and the public. The FBI employs community outreach specialists who establish partnerships with local citizens, host citizens' academies, and offer mentoring programs for children to help communities become "crime smart" (FBI—Community Outreach, n.d.). Their specialists, however, do not provide notifications or awareness briefings to the public upon the release of an ex-convict, let alone a convicted terrorist. DHS has expanded its "See Something, Say Something campaign," but has focused primarily on general suspicious activity reporting, not matters as specific as our subject of study. InfraGard chapters, regional partnerships between the FBI and the private sector "dedicated to sharing information and intelligence to prevent hostile acts against the United States," (InfraGard—Public Private Partnership —Federal Bureau of Investigation, n.d.), similarly do not share information when a convict is released from prison. Increased transparency of terrorism-related matters in the future could require the community outreach utility to provide an arena for more heightened awareness than what currently exists.

7.   Counsel

One obvious place to look for information is the individual's counsel of record. A convicted terrorist may continue to retain the services of legal representation during and after his sentence. It is logical to assume that the lawyer would know the location of his client after release from prison. We did not expect them to disclose any information about their clients, but for the sake of thoroughness, we made an effort to contact six attorneys.

We expected one of two responses: (1) *"My client is not a danger to society. He served his time and is moving on now with his life. He's smalltime/innocent/whatever else inconsequential and uninteresting for society at large. But I can't breach my privilege and give you personal information—I don't even know you."* (2) *"My client, as a convicted terrorist, has now been irrevocably and seriously stigmatized. He will require special protections in order to live in safety, and revealing his location would undermine those protections.*"

Five of the six attorneys responded to our inquiry. None of the representatives revealed the locations of their clients, and their responses did include our expected ones: "*My client... wishes to get along with his life and put his arrest and confinement behind him;*" "*...safety and privacy of my client and his family is my overriding concern;*" "*I am unable to accommodate your request.*" Two responses, though, were entirely unexpected: "*It is a stretch to lable* [sic] *(my client) as a 'convicted terrorist';*" "*We do not consider our client to be a convicted terrorist, the statute underlying his guilty plea notwithstanding. I think the govt [sic] would agree with our position (at least at the local level). Accordingly, his status is not relevant to your inquiry... Your inquiry relates to what you describe as the current residence of convicted terrorists, the proper characterization of our client's status is indeed a necessary predicate to your request.*"

The logic here is stunning. The latter two attorneys refused to engage us on grounds that their clients were not suitable subjects of study, this despite their conviction of terrorism-related crimes including conspiracy to aid the Taliban and providing material support to al Qaeda. We did not anticipate the strange hybrid that we received in these cases: "*My client is not a terrorist, and it's completely shocking for you to have asked or to have even called him a terrorist, but his location cannot be made public.*" This begs the question if the information might have been released had we not objectionably characterized their clients at the outset.

Though tangential to our inquiry, this introduces fascinating questions about what terrorism is. Brannan, Esler, and Strindberg caution against generalizing that all terrorists (or in our case, terrorism-related crimes) can be grouped together for analysis:

> The term ("terrorist") thus encompasses an enormous and highly disparate collection of groups and individuals... Simply categorizing them as "terrorists" does not make them remotely similar or even qualitatively or quantitatively comparable. (Brannan, Esler, & Strindberg, 2001, p. 19)

Even though DOJ and HRF appear to be clear on their respective definitions of terrorism, the ambiguity of the term introduces rich problems and potential obstacles to future programs and policies targeted toward our dataset of convicted and released terrorists. The inability to define terms even within one discipline (law) may be considerably disruptive as new policy is drafted. How can we determine requirements for sentencing or supervised release when such variance is evident?

8. Victims

Our research did not turn up the names of any first-order victims, as the plots in our dataset were (fortunately) disrupted before any direct harm occurred. However, the Office for Victims of Crime (OVC) within DOJ may provide an alternate channel for obtaining information about an ex-convict, as victims have rights to information about their assailants. The mission of OVC is to "enhance the Nation's capacity to assist crime victims by providing leadership and funding on behalf of crime victims" (What is the Office of Victims of Crime?, 2010). Contact with victims may be able to introduce opportunities to learn more about the path of convicted and released terrorists in the future.

B. INTERDISCIPLINARY COLLABORATION?

It is evident that multiple disciplines interact with a convicted terrorist—or have the opportunity to do so—during the transition from prison to society, including officials in the fields of policing, corrections, probation, witness protection, immigration, community outreach, law, and victims' advocacy. Lanes of responsibility have been established for the individual to swim through as he moves within the system. Some level of collaboration is marked by transitions from one phase in the process to the next, with probation officers generally serving as the primary agents responsible for monitoring the whereabouts of a released convict. Not discussed but also included as part of the

"intersection of prisoner reentry and civil society" are the issues of "public health, families and children, employment, housing and homelessness, youth development, and community policing" (J. Travis, 2006). These are the ripples we were hoping to find.

However, it may be misleading to call this interaction "interdisciplinary." The participants with a role in the path of the convicted terrorist contribute to a course of system that is rather linear. As Travis states:

> Police hand off arrests to prosecutors who in turn bring cases to court; in court, judges impose sentences on the guilty who in turn are sometimes sent off to prison. At the back end of this assembly line, prisoners are released from prison. (J. Travis, 2006, p. 333)

From an investigative standpoint, there is arguably no central entity or resource that has a holistic outlook on both the future of the released individual and the community he enters. In light of continued information sharing challenges between governmental disciplines, one may ask, where is the best place for a convicted and released terrorist's "case file" to reside? In other words, with whom does overall accountability lie? The subsequent findings and implications initiate the discourse for future actions.

V. FINDINGS

As we have embarked upon one of the greatest
social experiments of our time—the experiment of prisons
as our response to crime—we have forgotten
the iron law of imprisonment: they all come back.
Except for those few individuals who die in custody,
every person we send to prison returns to live with us.

– J. Travis, 2006, p. xvii

It has become evident through our research of released terrorists that we do not even understand the "the iron law of imprisonment," much less remember it. Our initial objective was to find individuals who were convicted of terrorism-related offenses, served time in prison, and were released into American communities. Upon finding these individuals, we presumed that we would learn about how the public is thinking and how impact is felt and addressed, as well as recognize novel and potentially useful patterns and relationships. We did not know *what* their effects would be, but we had preconceived notions that there would be *some* type of visible ripple in the pond or identifiable effect, whether it was constructive or galvanizing. Those ripples would be used to initiate the development of a blueprint for what was to follow. Defined indicators, clues, and trails could have been used to preempt prospective issues.

Instead, we could not find the pebble. Consequently, the answer to our first research question lingers. Ripple effects generated by the release of a convicted terrorist into a host American population are publicly unknown.

Much can be drawn from this overarching (non-)finding, however. The absence of information is fascinating in itself and can still be used to make sense of what we know at this point. By learning how criminals are processed, we identified topics along the terrorism continuum that require attention as homegrown terrorism continues to cause public concern. Even though we were unable to find evidence of noteworthy ripple effects, the issue is no less important and a different set of questions emerge.

Essentially, these results introduce the dialogue warranted by our second research question. There is much for America to consider after releasing those convicted of

61

terrorism-related crimes. Terrorists who are associated with more popularly recognized plots may invite increased visibility upon their release from prison in the years ahead. However, if they do not, and the event goes largely unrecognized by the government and the general public, it will be no less important to officials working in the justice, intelligence, and public policy disciplines, as well as community and business leaders. We identified four notable and recurring themes to describe present conditions:

- We do not know if convicted and released terrorists present a threat.
- Convicted terrorists are treated no differently from most convicted criminals.
- The American public knows very little about convicted and released terrorists.
- There is no defined entity responsible for convicted and released terrorists.

Given the shifting directions that have occurred in this research, it is helpful to understand in advance that the summaries of these findings are intended to be observational, as stated at the outset. Yet it becomes instantly obvious that future action based on these findings carry many implications that policy makers must consider. Therefore, rather than defining a departure point for next steps right now, the following chapter ("Implications") draws on these findings to introduce critical considerations as the narrative evolves. This was done to isolate the baseline of existing knowledge about convicted and released terrorists, because the subject is a new extension of the terrorism literature in the United States and requires a structured and methodical examination.

A. WE DO NOT KNOW IF CONVICTED AND RELEASED TERRORISTS PRESENT A THREAT

As previously stated, this research was conducted in an open source arena, and our outcomes and data might have been different if it had utilized classified or compartmentalized channels and resources. Importantly, though, our conclusion that the public does not presently have access to this information was derivable only through the limits we placed on the research design. Could convicted terrorists continue to be a threat after serving their prison term? It is debatable whether these individuals would return to a quiet civilian life or contribute to the war against America through different tactics or even with greater strength than they did prior to their sentencing.

We do know that there are places where released terrorists are welcomed into neighborhoods and even seen as "elder statesmen," as in Ireland and Indonesia. The following Indonesian example illustrates where the government has begun to recognize the emerging role of a convicted terrorist re-entering society:

> A former terror convict will always have a decision to make: to remain radical (or even to become more deeply radicalized) or to become more moderate, and work to reform his views and understanding of Islam and jihad. However, if we consider the bonds that are forged between terrorist convicts while incarcerated, it is clear that such men are more likely to remain radical than to become moderate, or reformed. These are the teachings to which they are exposed in prison and they are repeated and reinforced *when they rejoin their fellows outside. The incidence of former convicts who have gone on to commit further terrorism offenses provides ample proof that former terrorist prisoners do not or cannot let go of their established values.* (Emphasis added) (Ismail, 2010)

Assuming this is true, the obvious question is what the United States should be doing about a population with a nexus to national security that will remain within its borders after prison time is served. Could a convicted and released Islamist extremist in Indonesia share the same ideology or tendencies toward violence as a convicted and released Islamist extremist in the United States? Even though this foreign example is outside the scope of this research, the United States has an obligation to obtain these data to learn about convicted terrorists and establish grounds for comparison despite variances in cultures, laws, social norms, and public policies. This is a transnational issue that requires analysis across borders, especially since little is known about the subject in America.

We will not know if a threat is posed until time passes and data reflect it. Current figures on terrorist recidivism tend to be both anecdotal and nebulous, and have not been concentrated on terrorists imprisoned in the United States. Although the magnitude of the threat is unknown, a unique opportunity now exists to prepare for the prospect of nefarious activity. In the absence of weak signals, probabilities and assumptions can be used to stimulate a discussion of what approaches might be acceptable.

In general, public policy is constructed on justifiable grounds based upon actual patterns, data, events, and outcomes. The problem with proactive, preventive, and preemptive policy is that it often precedes the data. Society usually requires a regrettable event to serve as an impetus to create policy. For example, it took extreme consequences like the deaths of young children for sex offender legislation to achieve the visibility it has today. It will be similarly tragic if a convicted and released terrorist is responsible for the next terrorist attack.

Therefore, we will attempt to triangulate existing knowledge in order to speculate what paths the pending discourse will take. Fortunately, the unambiguous release date of a convicted terrorist provides the opportunity for reverse planning. This is one of the few times that the public may be able to foresee potential threats by individuals already associated with terrorism on some level.

B. CONVICTED TERRORISTS ARE TREATED NO DIFFERENTLY FROM MOST CONVICTED CRIMINALS

All terrorists are criminals, but not all criminals are terrorists. A review of the multiple disciplines that interact with convicts demonstrated that the organizational design of the system introduces questions that have not yet been answered. They are processed, they complete their sentence, and they are released. Should terrorists be treated differently from other convicts, with additional requirements? Is a finite post-release supervision term of two, three, or five years enough of a deterrent to future activity? Should conviction of a terrorism-related offense (either Category I or II) be seen as a "crime of violence," as covered by the Violent Crime Control and Law Enforcement Act of 1994? Even though conspiracy to launder money, violating export regulations, or contributing funds, goods, services to and for benefit of specially designated terrorists are not necessarily or inherently violent, do we automatically increase our risk by treating those ex-cons the same as those convicted of embezzlement, theft, or aiding and abetting the commission of a crime? Does the motivation and nexus to an extremist ideology or individual level of risk factor into what determines justice?

The absence of terrorist-specific policy requires the government to default to the larger framework provided by the American justice system. Hitherto, the United States has not had many terrorists in its universe of criminals. It comes therefore as no surprise that background discussions with representatives in multiple disciplines uncovered no procedural modifications triggered by the release of convicted terrorists.

Yet overall, criminal recidivism figures may cause reason for concern. If convicted terrorists mimic in any way the general population of convicted criminals, the American public may see reason for modifying the system. A 2002 Department of Justice study found:

> Of the 272,111 persons released from prisons in 15 States in 1994, an estimated 67.5% were rearrested for a felony or serious misdemeanor within 3 years, 46.9% were reconvicted, and 25.4% resentenced to prison for a new crime. (Langan & Levin, 2002; U.S. Department of Justice, Office of Justice Programs, Bureau of Justice Statistics, 2007)

How would the American public react if nearly half of the convicted terrorists in America were reconvicted after the completion of their sentence? It is too early to determine if terrorist recidivism is a high probability event, but even a fractional level should be of great concern and introduce more risk to the nation than what is created by other types of criminals. A terrorist carries a political agenda and threatens national security while the effects of a "garden variety" criminal are primarily focused on his victim and individual gain. As the United States continues to prosecute terrorists in the judicial system, it will be critical to prepare for the ramifications that come with potential acquittals, sentence commutations, and even international negotiations in the future. As national security is threatened from beyond and within U.S. boundaries, new policies could be used to further differentiate terrorists from other criminals to prevent against expansive ripple effects.

While existing laws may be sufficient for other criminals, differences presented by the terrorism issue may require a look from a separate vantage point. Public policy does exist to assist prisoners with reentry into American society upon their release. In his 2004 State of the Union Address, President George W. Bush sought increased assistance for ex-convicts:

Tonight I ask you to consider another group of Americans in need of help. This year, some 600,000 inmates will be released from prison back into society. We know from long experience that if they can't find work, or a home, or help, they are much more likely to commit crime and return to prison. So tonight, I propose a four-year, $300 million prisoner re-entry initiative to expand job training and placement services, to provide transitional housing, and to help newly released prisoners get mentoring, including from faith-based groups. America is the land of second chance, and when the gates of the prison open, the path ahead should lead to a better life. (G. W. Bush, 2004).

Did the President intend for the "land of second chance" to apply to all inmates, including those convicted of terrorism-related crimes who may continue to threaten national security? Could such a reentry initiative assist an ideologue whose actions may have been conducted to pursue a political agenda? Or is a more rigid "three strikes" policy (Marks, 2004) more suitable, in which repeat offenders are locked up permanently to deter violent crimes?

Society will need to decide if a terrorist can be defined as a special category of ex-convict during prison and after prison, and if he is worthy of a second chance of complete freedom. Should public policy be based upon what crime *has* been committed or what crime *might be* committed? This would depend upon any number of variables, including how morally repugnant the original crime is, the likelihood of recidivism, and the financial cost and security impact of recidivism, regardless of probability. While it may be argued that a policy can be crafted based upon recidivism, there is evidence to suggest that moral repugnance could factor into it as well. However, in his study of sex offender post-incarceration sanctions, Richard Wright challenges the legitimacy of basing policy on weak data and commonly held assumptions:

> Underlying all of the policy efforts to control sex offenders are several critical assumptions about their recidivism rates and patterns… A review of the literature on offender recidivism finds all of these assumptions are significantly flawed, raising questions about the empirical basis for sex offender laws. (Wright, 2008, p. 26)

The suggestion of post-incarceration sanctions for convicted terrorists could warrant similar criticism. Public awareness and political will are important factors that will dictate whether or not separate treatment is necessary for a different type of criminal, even if the data to support it is somewhat suspect. Right now, each factor is low.

C. THE PUBLIC KNOWS VERY LITTLE ABOUT CONVICTED AND RELEASED TERRORISTS

There was substantial media coverage of each defendant in our data set upon his capture, pending trial, and conviction that included background profiles, conspiracy details, statements by public officials, and community commentary in each case. However, the trail of information, and possibly interest, dried up upon conviction and was non-existent upon release.

Various possibilities exist to explain why the American public knows very little about Travis's iron law of imprisonment. We can only speculate, but by doing so we can identify what is required to address future policy effectively. To begin, the public may know very little because the topic simply has not surfaced as an issue requiring attention. Americans generally have confidence in the prison system and are forgiving toward an ex-convict who has paid his debt to society (thus, President Bush's description of America as "the land of second chance"). Release from prison is viewed as closure to the justice continuum, so post-prison life is rarely of public interest, except where the crime was heinous, likely to happen again, particularly violent, or some combination of factors.

A second reason why the public does not know much about ex-convicts is because information is challenging to obtain. The ability to find information is evidently crime-dependent. Sex offenders, especially pedophiles, are easy to track because there are public databases and search tools that can be used via the Internet to locate individuals by neighborhood. However, not much is available to the general population to know if a convicted terrorist lives nearby, unless the ex-convict was to openly declare his presence. These individuals do not make headlines in their post-prison lives in the same way they did when they were captured, convicted, and sentenced. Sometimes this is because they have kept a low profile; in other cases, they may have changed identity, either with or without police assistance.

Public records are scarce and limited for those who are interested in tracking these individuals. Indictments and court judgments are public documents, but neither provides a citizen with an individual's current location. Property tax records, Internet social networking websites, and pay-for-search investigative services are some of the few places that could be used to identify where an individual is residing, but not with much ease. Should it take a FOIA request or relationships with government insiders to learn about the location of an individual who was proven in a court of law to be guilty of a terrorism-related crime? Is it difficult by design to identify the location of ex-convicts so they are protected and alarm bells are not rung? Without increased transparency and focus on terrorism-related crimes, barriers to further knowledge will remain.

Another reason the public knows very little may be a testament to the prison system itself. Successes do not generate as much attention as failures do. It is possible that convicts were sent to correctional institutions, their behaviors were modified appropriately, and their return to society went unnoticed because acclimation was smooth and uneventful. Positive support networks have kept them in socially acceptable environments, and they have been able to maintain upstanding and lawful lifestyles away from the spotlight.

A fourth and much dimmer option is that convicts quietly returned to their circle of associates. They assimilated within the fringes of society from which they came, were granted a badge of honor for serving time in prison, and were welcomed back to a shadowy community within the United States. Connected to that scenario, it is also possible they departed the country voluntarily to achieve the same outcome. Severing their American ties would allow them to expand their foreign networks and influence. In either case, attempts at anonymity would be essential in order to avoid broad attention from the general public.

A final reason why the American public does not know much about released terrorists is because we may be too far out in front of the issue. There is not yet enough data, traction, or notoriety for public discourse. There has not been much time since 9/11, so the more serious, higher-profile terrorists have not completed their prison sentences and therefore have not yet "registered" on the public radar. Moreover, the concept of a released terrorist seems to be a nonsensical one to the general population, as Americans remain fixated on permanent solutions (death penalty, life in prison, deportation) even when it is clear that release from prison is inevitable. This is best evidenced by the August 5, 2010 front page of the satirical newspaper *The Onion*, as seen below in Figure 6. The concept of a released terrorist is so far-fetched that it is funny.

Figure 6.   Convicted and released terrorists become satirical (From: DHS Releases 5 Terrorists into U.S. to Test National Security, 2010)

Some terrorists are patiently serving their time of supervised release, so any ripple effects are not likely to occur until a date to be determined in the future. In any case, a defined timeframe as to when ripples could be expected is relative. Islamist extremists harbor resentment against the West for grievances incurred at the fall of the Ottoman Empire, so time, relatively speaking, is not a factor for them.

D. THERE IS NO DEFINED ENTITY RESPONSIBLE FOR CONVICTED AND RELEASED TERRORISTS

The final and most revealing finding of the research was that there was no evidence to suggest that anyone in particular is in charge of convicted and released terrorists once their supervised release ends. Should they be monitored for the rest of their lives? This issue, like many things governmental, stretches beyond the boundaries of one organization, fits under the disciplines and perspectives of multiple stakeholders, and introduces complexity, as well as complications to a situation with no simple solution. The linear yet distributed nature of the justice system enables a convict to pass through administrative processes from prison to probation and from probation to the public, in practically automated fashion. The system is programmed to do what it does, rather than retain much capacity for innovation, such as altering processes based upon the release of an ex-convict with potential national security consequences. There are no discernible incentives for interdisciplinary communication. Therefore, gaps may exist for an adversary to exploit during his reentry process. This should concern the national security apparatus, academia, and the general citizenry because it strikes each pillar of national preparedness. If a court conviction of a terrorist is one component of national response, then a strategy for the period that follows prison is essential to support recovery, as well as future prevention and protection efforts.

Thus, it appears that cases are handled individually instead of collectively. This is a difficulty in managing multidimensional issues across the government. A threat assessment issued in September 2010 by the Bipartisan Policy Center National Security Preparedness Group asked "[w]ho in fact has responsibility in the U.S. government to identify radicalization when it is occurring and then to interdict attempts at recruitment?" (Bergen & Hoffman, 2010). An initial list of suggested entities and disciplines included the FBI, state and local law enforcement, the Department of Homeland Security, the National Counterterrorism Center, and the Office of the Director of National Intelligence (Bergen & Hoffman, 2010). Bruce Hoffman, one of the report's co-authors, stated

…there is no single government agency responsible for deterring radicalization and terrorist recruitment. The terrorists may have found our Achilles heel--we have no way of dealing with this growing problem. (McCarter, 2010)

The same can be said of the post-prison population. There is no defined entity responsible for convicted and released terrorists, and the issue merits consideration as cases of homegrown terrorism are on the rise, and upon conviction, there exists additional opportunity for release from prison following sentencing. According to Brian Michael Jenkins of RAND:

> More cases of radicalization on U.S. soil were reported in 2009 than in any year since the September 11, 2001, terrorist attacks, but the number of cases, 13, hardly represents an explosion of radical fervor, especially since half of them involved lone individuals. *Whether this indicates a trend remains to be seen, but jihadist recruiting will continue….*
>
> Between September 11, 2001, and the end of 2009, a total of 46 cases of domestic radicalization and recruitment to jihadist terrorism were reported in the United States. In some cases, individuals living in the United States plotted to carry out terrorist attacks at home; some were accused of "providing material support to foreign terrorist organizations"… and some left the United States to join jihadist organizations abroad. All of these individuals can be called "homegrown terrorists."
>
> They demonstrate that radicalization and recruitment to terrorism can and does take place within the United States…. *They all meet one simple criterion for inclusion in the list: They have resulted in indictments, in the United States or abroad.* (Emphasis added) (Jenkins, 2010, p. 1)

A policy discussion about convicted and released terrorists is therefore unavoidable.

THIS PAGE INTENTIONALLY LEFT BLANK

VI. IMPLICATIONS

Until we have a genuine dialogue on these core issues,
any solution we come up with will be partial at best
and inadequate to address the challenge....
Clearly, a new type of entry point for collective action is needed,
one that is available to all the stakeholders, local and global.

– Gerencser et al., 2008, pp. 42–43

A.   LOOKING AHEAD

This research was started to generate interest about an issue not yet on the forefront of homeland security discourse in the United States. Even though we failed to locate convicted and released terrorists and feel their ripple effects, we identified evidence of the population, learned about the system that processes them, and developed four findings that can be used to initiate a "genuine dialogue" for analysis and action. Background discussions with current and former public officials revealed no existing strategy focused on convicted and released terrorists from the following organizations:

- Bureau of Alcohol, Tobacco and Firearms
- Central Intelligence Agency
- Defense Intelligence Agency
- Department of Homeland Security
- Federal Bureau of Investigation
- Federal Bureau of Prisons
- Federal Emergency Management Association
- National Institute of Justice
- Naval Criminal Investigative Service
- Transportation Security Administration
- U.S. Attorney Offices
- U.S. Marshals Service
- U.S. Military Academy
- U.S. Probation and Pretrial Services

73

- U.S. Secret Service
- State and local law enforcement

For this reason, we must begin to explore possible options for the future and the implications of proceeding with those options. This brings us to our second research question: what issues should America consider after releasing someone convicted of terrorism-related crimes?

B.   FIRST OPTIONS

The following series of discussions should be used to initiate an informal, yet sophisticated policy dialogue. These discussions will become more robust upon the emergence of data, as patterns are detected. Those patterns will then be used to determine the costs and benefits of pursuing each action. Four alternatives are presented for discussion: maintain the status quo, assess individual risk, lengthen detainment beyond the prison sentence, and introduce monitoring.

These are not the only options, and they are not mutually exclusive. One of the common threads that weave them together is risk of radicalization. The ultimate decision to pursue one direction will be based on perceived or actual risk. Even if the population of convicted terrorists is relatively small compared with the population of other types of convicts, there is still a responsibility to learn about it. As Bergen and Hoffman state:

> While it must be emphasized that the number of U.S. citizens and residents affected or influenced in this manner remains extremely small, at the same time the sustained and growing number of individuals heeding these calls (of terrorist radicalization and recruitment) is nonetheless alarming. (Bergen & Hoffman, 2010, p. 30)

Therefore, following the summary of alternatives, we expand our review of literature and discuss a set of core questions that connect convicted and released terrorists to the broader dialogue of homegrown terrorism and radicalization.

1.   Maintain the Status Quo

Doing nothing is certainly an option. While the inclination to act for the sake of acting may expedite the discourse, opponents may resist in the absence of justifiable data, available time, and adequate resources. Eric Janus, Professor of Law at William Mitchell College of Law, contends that there has been too much "radical prevention" in the United States and cites preventive measures against sex offenders and terrorists as swinging the balance between security and liberty too strongly toward security:

> First, radical prevention seeks to intervene where there is some sort of "propensity" or risk of *future* harm, whereas routine prevention responds to actual or attempted harm. Second, radical prevention operates by substantially curtailing people's liberty *before* harm results, whereas in routine prevention individuals suffer deprivations of liberty only after actual harm is done or attempted. (Janus, 2004, p. 2)

In other words, by operating more reactively, there is less likelihood to impede upon individual freedoms entitled to members of the general public. However, those who believe that released criminals have a greater likelihood than other citizens of committing a criminal act, and that a conviction warrants punishment beyond prison, may regard Janus's "radical prevention" as merely proactive work. Nonetheless, Janus further argues that moving quickly without adequate evidence is not desirable. He quotes Rose:

> [O]nce it seems that today's decisions can be informed by calculations about tomorrow, we can demand that calculations about tomorrow should and must inform all decisions made today. The option of acting in the present in order to manage the future rapidly mutates into something like an obligation. (Janus, 2004, p. 34)

The problem is that "calculations about tomorrow," which are based on risk, will always remain unclear. Policy is often prepared as a product that follows a sequence of events rather than intuition; although convicted terrorists are being released from prison, the absence of ripples may provide little reason to initiate transformation of any kind.

Until communities identify with a measurable impact caused by this population, the status quo could prevail. It is possible to purport that terms of supervised release are working effectively, and individual behaviors shift toward inactivity or dormancy, rather than any type of visible activity.

Another rationale to defend the status quo is to avoid making a mountain out of a molehill. Implementing new policy may create unanticipated consequences, triggering new threats and stymieing potential stakeholders. As courses of action are explored, it is important to exercise process discipline effectively because of the timing associated with this issue. This research so far has demonstrated that convicted and released terrorists do not appear to be attracting any attention. The general public has shown limited if any interest in them. It is possible that our population may not turn out to be a central front for the study of homegrown terrorism. Accordingly, it is critical to ensure that new ripples are not inadvertently caused by introducing a rigorous policy debate at the wrong time. U.S. Army General David Petraeus explains the consequences of action in Iraq:

> Realize that we are in a struggle for legitimacy that will be won or lost in the perception of the Iraqi people. Every action taken by the enemy and our forces has implications in the public arena. Develop and sustain a narrative that works and continually drive the themes home through all forms of media. (Hoffman, 2009, pp. 367–368)

Therefore, it may be prudent to maintain the status quo and provide each ex-convict with a clean slate rather than introducing new policy of any kind. After all, it can be argued that ex-convicts, including those convicted of terrorism-related crimes, have completely paid their debts to society.

2.   Assess Individual Risk

Since the risk of a repeat terrorist may differ from the risk of a repeat criminal, the punitive actions offered by the justice system may need to be reconsidered. In other words, while broad policy need not be introduced, it may still be necessary to ensure that convicted terrorists are assessed on an individual basis prior to release in order to determine what level of risk is appropriate for the individual and the community to which he enters.

Is one "type" of terrorist riskier than another? We conducted our research of convicted terrorists based on the description provided by HRF, and also previously noted that DOJ recognizes two tiers of terrorism-related crimes. However, a more targeted approach may be needed to parse out which terrorists are riskier than others, as broadly generalizing "all terrorists" may be too simple. In *From the Terrorist's Point of View*, Fathali Moghaddam identifies:

Nine specialized roles among terrorists: (A) source of inspiration (B) strategist (C) networker (D) expert (E) cell manager (F) local agitator and guide (G) local cell member (H) fodder, and (I) fund-raiser. (Moghaddam, 2006, p. 100)

Does or should the role of a terrorist correlate to the post-prison measures imposed upon him? For instance, how would the risk presented by a strategist with broad influence be compared to the risk presented by a local cell member or fund-raiser? Would it be easier to assess the level of radicalization presented by an individual who is a source of inspiration and espouses extremist views versus someone who writes a check and perhaps holds a more moderate perspective? Moghaddam recognizes that these roles are not necessarily mutually exclusive of each other, as "in many instances, one individual will fill more than one individualized role" (Moghaddam, 2006, p. 100). If such is the case, those convicted of terrorism-related crimes in lower level roles like those we tried to follow may require closer and longer observation before they have the opportunity after prison to shift from one function to a riskier one, especially if prison exacerbated any existing grievances.

The challenge lies in the reality that a small group (such as 21 individuals sentenced to 5–8 years in prison, or even 160 individuals not sentenced to life in prison) may not necessarily yield enough material for dividing data into units appropriate for trending or analysis. However, we can begin to ask the relevant questions that factor into the discussion about risk.

There is significant merit to triaging individual cases based on risk, because different persons may not only hold different roles, but they may also be at different stages in the radicalization process. In their well-circulated assessment, Silber and Bhatt of the New York Police Department (NYPD) Intelligence Division delineate the four phases of radicalization: pre-radicalization, self-identification, indoctrination, and jihadization (Silber & Bhatt, 2007, p. 19). As the report states:

Each of these phases is unique and has specific signatures associated with it. All individuals who begin this process do not necessarily pass through all the stages and many, in fact, stop or abandon this process at different points. Moreover, although this model is sequential, individuals do not always follow a perfectly linear progression. However, individuals who do pass through this entire process are quite likely to be involved in a terrorist act. (Silber & Bhatt, 2007, p. 19)

Accordingly, we do not know yet what formulas, sequences, phases, or other schemata can be suggested for an individual after prison time is served. Silber and Bhatt deduced their findings from examining multiple, detailed cases. While it may or may not align perfectly with the trajectory of someone released from prison, we must decide whether to use an existing methodology or theoretical framework to evaluate a convicted terrorist, or create a new one based on empirical data.

Individuals convicted of terrorism-related offenses presumably reached some level of inspiration to participate in illegal activity. Yet the effect of imprisonment is hard to predict. The question then is whether their time in prison *advanced* their progression through the aforementioned stages of radicalization toward "accept(ing) their individual duty to participate in jihad and self-designat(ing) themselves as holy warriors or mujahedeen" (Silber & Bhatt, 2007, p. 7), *reduced* their propensity for further involvement as the correctional system was designed to do, or created some other possibility that has not yet been determined.

Thus, it may be beneficial to evaluate cases individually, rather than establishing a course of direction painted in broad strokes and modifying systemic procedures. A programmatic solution may be too burdensome. Distinguished social psychologist Philip Zimbardo, notably recognized for his Stanford Prison Experiment in 1971 and his work following the exposure of detainee treatment at the Abu Ghraib prison, weighs solutions by addressing individual versus group remedies in his 2007 best seller, *The Lucifer Effect: Understanding How Good People Turn Evil*:

> 'While a few bad apples might spoil the barrel (filled with good fruit/people), a barrel filled with vinegar will always transform sweet cucumbers into sour pickles—regardless of the best intentions, resilience, and genetic nature of those cucumbers.' So, does it make more sense to spend our resources on attempts to identify, isolate, and destroy the few bad apples or to learn how vinegar works so that we can teach cucumbers how to avoid undesirable barrels? (Zimbardo, 2007, p. 47)

Can we just focus on individuals and keep them away from what is deemed undesirable? Or is it worth the effort to overhaul the justice system or reform society and introduce new policy? As an FBI spokesperson stated following the arrest of a Pakistani-American suspected of plotting to bomb the Washington, D.C., commuter rail system, the Bureau

> ...does not investigate communities or mosques but individuals. 'We are going to go within constitutional parameters where we need to go and talk to people we need to talk to,' said spokeswoman Katherine Schweit. 'But we are not looking to infiltrate anything other than individuals looking to harm others.' (Wan, 2010)

3.   Lengthen Detainment Beyond the Prison Sentence

If we recognize that an individualized approach to address convicted and released terrorists is more viable than a programmatic solution, more information is needed to understand what an "acceptable" level of risk is. Would a poor performance on an individualized assessment require the government to detain a convicted terrorist beyond his court-issued prison sentence?

Such a scenario provides us with a third possibility. Lengthening detention of those convicted of terrorism-related crimes may reduce recidivism and ripples throughout the community. It is not farfetched to believe that failing to act may be perceived as weak policy, and decision makers may subsequently implement such a measure to preempt known and unknown risk. While that risk may appear subjective to the general public, it would be the responsibility of the public officials to communicate why such a decision is not fear-mongering, discriminatory, or frivolous.

Because post-prison activities for terrorists convicted in U.S. courts are not known, there may be a better chance of preventing a future attack by detaining them longer, whether they are convicted in a civilian or military court. For example, regarding the sentencing of alleged al-Qaida militant Omar Khadr, retired U.S. Army Sergeant Layne Morris stated:

They ought to lock him up until he's no longer a threat, and if that's for the rest of his life, so be it... Knowing the facts of the case, I would think your average American would be disappointed that somebody who had demonstrated the capacity and the willingness to kill American soldiers would get a mere eight years... That seems short to me... He should get 20 years and then be evaluated to see if he is still a security threat... And if he is, then he can do another 20 years. (Fox, 2009)

However, does a longer sentence correlate to a greater probability of success after ex-convict is eventually released from prison? Are there notable breakeven points that can be used to indicate when an individual has moved from ideologue to moderate to 'heeled?' In their presentation to the INTERPOL 79th General Assembly, researchers of the Qatar International Academy for Security Studies (QIASS) Countering Violent Extremism (CVE) Risk Reduction Project (hereafter, "Risk Reduction Project") stated that with detainment,

> There is also potential opportunity. Some terrorists who are detained have their first experience in a while of being separated from the collective influence and environment of other extremists... Sometimes they become receptive to alternative ideas or willing to engage critically in examining their justifications... upon release, the now 'former' terrorist can be a credible voice among active militants. (Risk Reduction for Countering Violent Extremism, 2010, p. 5)

On the other hand, does an extreme ideologue become more agitated or radicalized by serving more time? Does it delay the inevitable, if there is any plan at all to release a convict before he dies? The Risk Reduction Project also describes capture and detention as "just tools; they are not long-term solutions" (Risk Reduction for Countering Violent Extremism, 2010). Again, some type of risk assessment may be required to determine when release is appropriate.

Is there precedent for the use of extended detainment? The most applicable example comes from a type of crime that has been ruled so egregious that it has been given its own framework for jurisprudence. The 2010 Supreme Court case of *U.S. v. Comstock* revealed in a 7–2 verdict that "government officials can detain 'sexually dangerous' offenders even after their federal prison terms have been completed" (Barnes, 2010; United States v. Comstock et al. No. 08–1224, 2010). Social acceptance of extended sentencing does exist as the ostracization of sex offenders has been upheld through legislation and in the courts. Janus describes this type of sexual predator law as a "commitment law," which is

> ... aimed at sex offenders who are completing their prison sentences, but are judged "too dangerous" to be released. The laws are limited to offenders who not only pose a risk of future sexual harm, but also have some form of "mental disorder." Like conventional mental illness commitment laws, the predator laws are deemed civil not criminal in nature. Confinement is not in prisons, but in secure treatment facilities. Commitments are for an indeterminate period, ending only when the individual is no longer dangerous. (Janus, 2004, p. 8)

Could such confinement be applied in an analogous manner to allow for the rehabilitation of a terrorist? Should a separate framework be established? Under the ex post facto clause of the U.S. Constitution, punishment cannot be retroactively increased after conviction. Legally speaking, punishment cannot be increased after conviction. Therefore, lengthening detainment of a convicted terrorist would need to be conducted as some kind of civil commitment scheme like that used for sex offenders.

How would the evaluation of such status be measured? Do terrorists have mental disorders? Hoffman states, "Contrary to both popular belief and media depiction, most terrorism is neither crazed nor capricious. Rather, terrorist attacks are generally both premeditated and carefully planned" (Hoffman, 2006, p. 229).

While Guantánamo detainees are not part of this analysis because they have not yet been convicted of terrorism-related crimes, discussions from within the Obama Administration introduce parallel arguments about both individual risk assessments and lengthened detainment. In December 2010, the Administration spoke about issuing an executive order that "would establish something like a parole board to evaluate whether each detainee poses a continued threat, or whether he can be safely transferred to another country" (Savage, 2010). Questions posed by a White House source could just as well be posed for convicted terrorists already serving time in American prisons (not as an increase to criminal punishment, but as a civil commitment scheme) if their detainment were to be extended beyond the prison sentence:

81

Are they (detained) for the rest of their lives? What's the review mechanism? How impartial is it? Do they have a chance to contest it? All of that stuff has to be answered. And we have been working on an executive order laying out these elements. (Finn & Kornblut, 2010)

It will be critical to comprehend what prospective ripple effects may be felt by government, the individual, and society prior to proceeding.

Hence, the decision to hold convicted terrorists until they pass some type of assessment would be a controversial one, as it is already notorious for those who have not even seen trial. Civil libertarians argue that justice is served upon the completion of a prison sentence, and also communicate their fear of increased federal power. As Wendy Kaminer argued in *The Atlantic*:

> Much damage has been done. Federal criminal jurisdiction has expanded dramatically in the last few decades, with the blessings of conservatives and liberals alike. Now, thanks to the ruling in *U.S. v Comstock*, that power seems practically infinite: federal authorities can *imprison people indefinitely on suspicions of future dangerousness*. It's not just suspected sex offenders or terrorists who are at risk. (Emphasis added) (Kaminer, 2010)

The concept of a slippery slope could apply to other (perceived) risky groups by lengthening the detainment of any targeted population. In a 2002 piece, Clark McCauley addresses the concerns of the slippery slope to the field of terrorism studies, foreshadowing events that publicly surfaced:

> Since September 11, there have already been suggestions from reputable people that U.S. security forces may need to use torture to get information from suspected terrorists. This is the *edge of a slope* that leads down and away from the rule of law and the presumption of innocence. (Emphasis added) (McCauley, 2002, p. 16)

Such an argument could be made about extending prison sentences. Janus argues that the creation of a separate framework constituting any extended detainment is an "expansive alternate and degraded system of justice" (Janus, 2004, p. 2) that is based on "the risk they pose, not their guilt" (Janus, 2004, p. 21). He likens such action to racial discrimination laws in which "outsider group's rights were reduced in order to prevent some (imagined) future harm to the larger society" (Janus, 2004, p. 11). Wright states that there may be societal acceptance of withholding the rights of 21st century terrorists, as well:

> American society generally disproves of detaining someone for crimes they might or might not commit, yet we seem to tolerate preventive detention for sex offenders *and terrorists*. (Emphasis added) (Wright, 2008, p. 41)

Does the use of the term "terrorists" mean that detention is tolerable for those who have even been convicted, sentenced, and released? It is critical to bear in mind the difference between enemy combatants and convicted terrorists as described in Chapter II. Enemy combatants were captured, but not tried or judged, while convicted terrorists were captured, tried, ruled guilty, and sentenced to prison by a court of law. Wright and Janus may find parallels between the outsider groups held at Guantánamo Bay (Janus, 2004, p. 6) and the Japanese detained during World War II. (Janus, 2004, p. 11). However, once a prison sentence for a convicted felon is finished, the argument to extend detention weakens.

Lengthening detainment beyond a prison sentence may be construed as problematic because it is based on the possibility of a future act, rather than an actual act. Such an action is an example of "pre-crime," which McCulloch says:

> ...*links coercive state actions to suspicion* without the need for charge, prosecution or conviction. It also includes measures that expand the remit of the criminal law to include activities or associations that are *deemed to precede the substantive offence targeted for prevention*. ... the shift to pre-crime embodies a trend towards integrating national security into criminal justice along with a temporal and geographic shift that encompasses a blurring of the borders between the states' internal and external coercive capacities. The counter-terrorism framework incorporates and combines elements of criminal justice and national security, giving rise to a number of tensions. (Emphasis added) (McCulloch, 2009)

At the very least, convicted terrorists already have some historical record of committing an illegal act. However, should conviction of a certain crime be sufficient to warrant further detention, in anticipation of a not-yet-committed offense? The "tension" between criminal justice and national security that McCulloch describes is quite evident. Such is the challenge faced by policy makers who are charged with identifying what steps are appropriate to address this facet of homegrown terrorism.

4.   Introduce Monitoring

Since increasing sentencing requirements places additional strain on the prison system, further imprisonment may not be viable. According to the Police Executive Research Forum, overcrowding prisons and limited resources require

> …innovative approaches to address the reentry challenge facing the law enforcement community as states address budget shortfalls by cutting corrections budgets, expanding parole and early release programs, and modifying sentencing laws… (Executive Session—Prisoner Reentry, Oct. 7, n.d.)

Therefore, somewhere between the status quo and indefinite detainment lies the option to provide convicted terrorists with restricted freedom after prison, to strike a balance between liberty and security. But was a balance intended to be struck? This dialogue is not new, as Benjamin Franklin said centuries ago: "They who can give up essential liberty to obtain a little safety, deserve neither liberty nor safety." (B. Franklin & W. T. Franklin, 1818, p. 270). General Michael Hayden, director of the Central Intelligence Agency under President George W. Bush from 2006–2009, was asked about this balance, but instead used the term "tradeoffs." He commented:

> If you look at the foundation documents and see why it is we have organized government among men… it is to preserve life, liberty, and the pursuit of happiness. And I will equate 'life' with 'security'… Based on the Declaration of Independence, I'd put security, life, and the pursuit of happiness are all values… it's not 'security' and 'values.' At our very essence, our foundation documents teach us that they are *all* values and we make tradeoffs among them all the time… when people say it's a false choice between liberty and security, I think what they're actually telling you is 'it's a hard choice and I'd rather not make it.' (Hayden, 2010).

Should a convicted terrorist be provided with all liberties rightfully accorded to him after his release, or is some component of freedom permanently forfeited based upon his actions? What is the problem with monitoring an individual who "pursues happiness" by maintaining the life of a model citizen after prison? Can his debt to society truly be repaid, or should his activities be tracked by being placed on a shorter leash? The USA PATRIOT Act allows for an indefinite term of supervised release, but we identified individuals convicted of terrorism-related crimes who received fewer than five years of monitoring. Is this enough?

The United States has already developed a no-fly list to secure the aviation transportation system, but should known terrorists be subjected to additional restrictions to protect more than the flying public and transportation infrastructure? Peter Kratcoski, following a meeting on the topic of "Terrorist Victimization: Prevention, Control, and Recovery" at the United Nations Center in Vienna, Austria recognized that "Exchanges of information on effective methods of obtaining information on the activities of known terrorists and containing their efforts are vitally important" (Kratcoski, 2001, p. 472). Does this type of "exchange" include members of the general public as a contributor or stakeholder? On the other hand, is this just intended for intelligence or law enforcement purposes? Travis's description of a "stubborn fact" of reentry may lay the groundwork for extra action. He states:

> The odds against successful reentry are daunting…. In crafting policies to improve the chances of successful reentry, we must confront this stubborn fact: under current conditions, most prisoners will fail to lead law-abiding lives when they return home. (J. Travis, 2006, p. 87)

Is this a risk worth taking with convicted terrorists? If it is common knowledge that most prisoners will fail, should the type of conviction be a factor in determining what actions should be taken upon their release? Such differentiation may produce grounds for introducing monitoring of convicted terrorists as a legitimate policy option. If the release of any convicted terrorist is predicated on the condition that the he never again participate in activities or associate with individuals that undermine the security of the United States, the use of supervision may be necessary (Cannon, 2009). As a colleague of the author proposes, and perhaps addressing the tradeoff previously suggested by General Hayden:

Effective supervision can best be accomplished by the U. S. Probation Office, a branch of the U.S. Court system. Detainees who violate the conditions of probation should be subject to returning to prison. ... By creating conditions of probation for detainees and securing international cooperation, any potential threat these former detainees present to the United States can be mitigated. (Cannon, 2009)

Actions can be taken that make sense to society, or make sense to the convicted terrorist. We can keep tabs on where he is, and/or we can punish, incentivize, or disincentivize his behavior to make an example out of the individual. However, it is not so simple. Such an effort would require resources, perhaps more than those utilized by law enforcement as well. In their reflection of a conference hosted by the International Peace Institute, Fink and Hearne recognize the challenges of monitoring people:

The difficulty of monitoring participants following the conclusion of a program impacts the ability to measure success, and is not unrelated to challenges concerning resources and capacity. That is, not all programs have the capacity to track the behavior and movements of participants after they leave the program; this expense is particularly felt in NGO led programs since their government-run counterparts have access to the security and intelligence mechanisms of the state. While this access is helpful on a number of levels, it also raises concerns regarding civil liberties. Monitoring is important, especially given the dangers of recidivism, requiring sophisticated and complex programs or parole-like mechanisms for postrelease support and assistance. (Fink & Hearne, 2008, p. 13)

Some crimes have been deemed so egregious by the general public that supervision is demanded and normative. Sex offenders are frequently recognized as the worst of the worst criminals. Wright registers their place relative to other crimes, including terrorism:

There is little argument that sex offenders viewed as *more dangerous criminals than terrorists*, murderers, gang leaders, mobsters, arsonists, drug dealers, and white-collar criminals. Whether one believes that sex offenders—the heterogeneous group that they are—deserve this level of control and scrutiny is for the reader to decide. (Emphasis added) (Wright, 2008, pp. 49–50)

We do not yet know if convicted terrorists rank comparably to sex offenders in the hierarchy of morally repugnant actors. The United States does not have scalable context between the two types of criminals, as there are 674,000 sex offenders (America's Unjust Sex Laws, 2009), in the country compared with hundreds of terrorists. Substantive data, future context, and identification of ripples will determine the extent of applicable stigmata. While there is a certain role for contrition and repentance in the United States, their application will depend upon whether or not the general public sees a convicted terrorist as a looming threat.

This will be contingent upon what is agreed upon as "terrorist activity," just as the Adam Walsh Child Protection and Safety Act of 2006 established three tiers of sex offenses that correlate to public registration requirements (Wright, 2008, p. 32). It has taken years for the expansive and layered structure to take shape. However, now a multilayered apparatus exists for this special subset of the criminal population, including registration with local law enforcement, community notification, national database classifications, electronic monitoring, and residency restrictions and exclusionary zones (Wright, 2008, pp. 29–46).

Under Megan's Law, citizens are informed of sexual predators living in their communities through registration requirements. This framework is described by Janus:

> Although varying from state to state, these laws require released sex offenders to register with local authorities, and adopt some form of community notification regarding the presence, and sometimes the level of risk, of offenders in the community. (Janus, 2004, p. 8)

Implementation of a terrorist registry would trigger questions—both for the individual and society at large. Would all categorizations of terrorist activity warrant listing on a neighborhood terrorist registry, or would rules vary for the Type I and Type II terrorist designations that were created by DOJ? Could adversaries misuse a registry as a recruitment directory? Could it enflame a released terrorist and serve and grounds for another grievance that justifies his ideology? Or could it shame an ex-convict so much that it dissuades him from returning to illegal activity?

Shaming via public disclosure may be a considerable deterrent. Such tactics are nothing new, as evidenced centuries ago during the Middle Ages. Charivari, "was a ritual used by medieval and early modern Europeans to chastise community members who failed to conform to social expectations" (Charivari, n.d.). As Travis states, "we must first recognize the existence, through the history of Western civilization, of a profoundly deep, culturally embedded impulse to demonize those who have violated the law" (J. Travis, 2006, p. 253). Does demonization help increase public safety?

Any label, visible or invisible, provides grounds for an assortment of new ripples. The use of a public database may serve as a mechanism for behavior modification of the ex-convict, and possibly those who formerly associated with him. To date, one does not exist. According to Frank J. Cilluffo, former Special Assistant to the President for Homeland Security and Director of the Homeland Security Policy Institute at The George Washington University, there is "no database… to track inmates after release or to identify inmates associated with radical groups…" (Prison Radicalization, 2006).

Victims groups may experience feelings of "cynicism and lack of faith in the established social order and judicial system on the part of citizens" (Subramanian, 2000, p. 4). They may be

> …intimidated by the terrorists, and government agents attempting to control the terrorism may impose restrictions on the citizens' abilities to move about freely or compromise their human rights through interrogation efforts to discover the identities or locations of the terrorists. (Kratcoski 2001, p. 470)

The introduction of new monitoring capabilities and procedures undoubtedly describes these types of restriction. Therefore, branding convicted terrorists with a proverbial Scarlet Letter may provide them with feelings of justice being served. On the other hand, victims' trauma may be exacerbated by knowing the location of a freed conspirator. Moreover, it is possible that citizen activism may go too far. Immediately after 9/11, law-abiding Muslims, as well as Sikhs mistaken for Muslims, were targets of assault and other vigilante "justice" (Man Questioned in Shooting Death of Sikh, 2001).

Despite popular support for monitoring sexual predators, lawsuits are still filed against state policies, as seen from Connecticut (Connecticut's Sex Offender Website Registry Violates Rights, Court Rules, 2001) to Indiana (Federal Court Sides with ACLU In Sex Offender Consent-to-Search Case, 2008) to Nevada (The ACLU of Nevada Wins

Temporary Stay of New Sex Offender Laws, 2008). Many continue to argue that justice is served upon the completion of a prison sentence, and changing the rules for one population could lead to a slippery slope for other populations.

To move forward with any type of restriction necessitates an understanding of its intended and unintended impact. Is there recourse for false positives? Can an individual ever be removed from a public list? The no-fly list has been subject to public scrutiny over matters of intelligence, civil liberties, and foreign policy. Might similar or further unintended consequences arise from the monitoring of released terrorists? Zimbardo asks a collection of critical questions for consideration:

> Social psychologists... prefer to begin their search for meaning (of explanations of culpability, illness, and sin) by asking the 'What questions': *What conditions could be contributing to certain reactions? What circumstances might be involved in generating behavior? What was the situation like from the perspective of the actors?* (Zimbardo, 2007, pp. 7–8)

The "situation" from the perspective of the convicted terrorist in America appears to be a quiet one, as no public policy exists to monitor his movements. Thus far, our research shows there is no visible "situation" at this time. How would the environment change if monitoring and public shaming are central facets of the post-prison life of a convicted terrorist? Could the release of a higher profile terrorist in the next ten years create a situation requiring new policy that reduces the level of privacy afforded him under the existing system?

Travis describes the public challenge for released convicts as twofold:

> Our challenge is to define those mutual obligations in ways that recognize the distinct interests of the returning prisoner and society. The prisoner's interests are clear—connecting with family, health care, employment, housing, and community institutions. Society has important interests as well—reducing crime, promoting successful family reunification, and security employment and improving health outcomes for the population of former prisoners. (J. Travis, 2006, p. 55)

Are these broad interests the same for those associated with terrorism-related crimes? How much do health care, employment, or community institutions matter to an individual committed to changing the political structure of the society he reenters? Does society truly want to reunify these individuals with family members who may be the reason they committed an illegal act in the first place? The terrorism literature may help us here. By understanding the effects of an individual on society and society on an individual, we can explore the considerations that will be required to address these individuals in the United States.

C.   RISK REDUCTION

American society will debate the appropriate course of action for convicted and released terrorists in the United States, whether it be to maintain the status quo, assess individual risk, lengthen detainment beyond the prison sentence, introduce monitoring, or identify a completely different alternative. For example, a law enforcement or intelligence officer may leverage an ex-convict for intelligence purposes or track him upon his release from prison for an extended period of time to protect the public against recidivism. A social worker may invest time into studying what causal factors led the individual to conduct the act in the first place, to prevent it from happening again. Reduced risk and public peace comprise the desired end state for each discipline, but the means by which society achieves it varies.

Thus, it is helpful to learn about the variables that underlie suggested options from the social sciences so the foundation for preventive strategy is understood. Because the raw data on convicted terrorists is limited, we have used secondary sources from which to extrapolate.

Situational factors may present some commonalities between groups or individuals. But as Davis and Jenkins state, "Terrorists are not a single foe, and no simple theory of deterrence can possibly apply to the spectrum that ranges from anti-U.S. or anti-Israeli 'martyrs' to members of American right-wing militias" (Davis & Jenkins, 2002, p. 7). Similarly, there is not one model that can be used to predict the effectiveness of mitigation measures or foresee the post-prison lives of convicted and released terrorists. Such an effort is not achievable, as described by Davis and Cragin of RAND:

In social science, it is seldom possible to make strong predictions... A better aspiration is to "improve the odds" of correct diagnosis and prescription and to lay the groundwork for rapid adaptations in response to more information... He who 'bets the farm' on the predictions of a model... is likely to lose that farm—if not the first time, then the second or third. (Noricks, Helmus, Paul, Berrebi, Jackson, Gvineria, Egner, & Bahney, 2009, p. 1)

The focus of our research can be seen at intersection of the fields of anthropology, economics, geography, history, political science, psychology, and sociology, as well as cross-cutting fields of terrorism studies, criminology, organization theory, and policy analysis (Noricks, Helmus, Paul, Berrebi, Jackson, Gvineria, Egner, & Bahney, 2009, p. 5). As the dataset grows over time, we will be able to tell if existing models can be extended and applied to the population.

Helmus provides a clear, succinct summary in the RAND study of what motivates an individual to engage in terrorism, as presented in Figure 7 (Noricks, Helmus, Paul, Berrebi, Jackson, Gvineria, Egner, & Bahney, 2009, pp. xxv, 95).

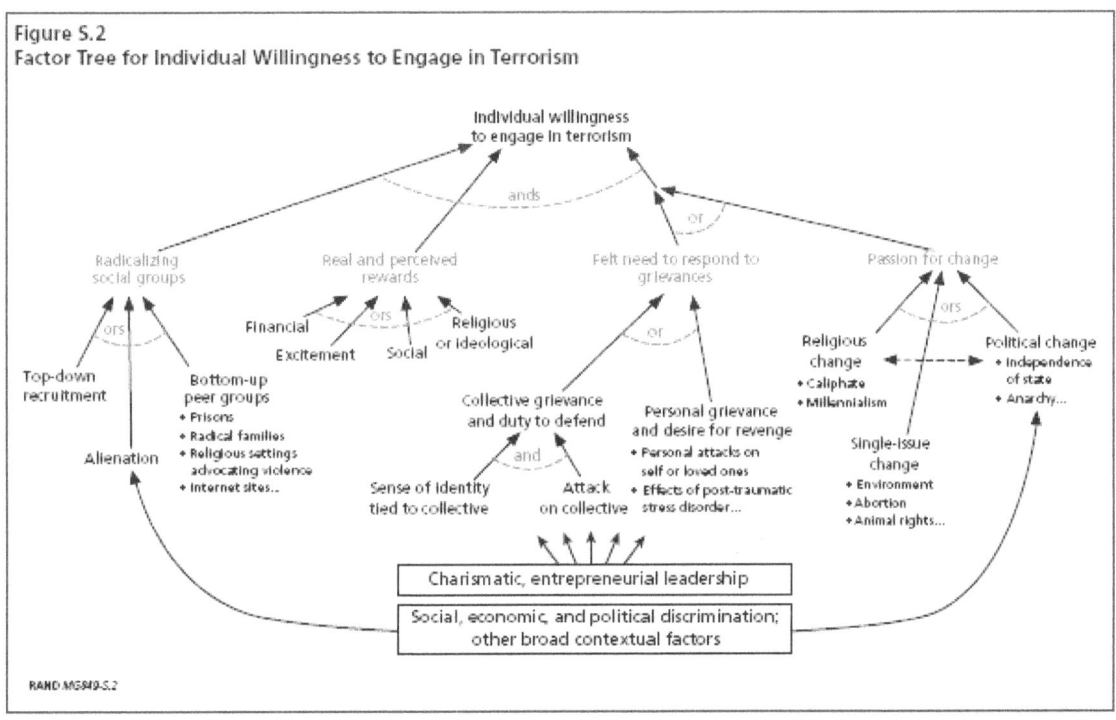

Figure 7.   Factor Tree for Individual Willingness to Engage in Terrorism (From: Noricks et al., 2009, p. xxv)

91

There are multiple relationships between the factors that would cause an individual to participate in terrorism, to include radicalizing social groups, real and perceived awards, felt need to respond to grievances, and passion for change (Noricks et al., 2009, pp. 94, 96). Each factor provides context and motivation behind the willingness of an individual to act. This framework was developed to depict the front end of the terrorism continuum, and issues leading up to an incident.

However, it may also be applied to assess the issues leading up to *another* incident, as the individual profile for a convicted and released terrorist has not yet been established. A court conviction and prison sentence for a terrorism-related crime could alter the strength of these same factors, which can then be used to inform us how individuals *return* to the same loop of progression toward radicalization. Since we already know that they had some nexus to terrorism, there ought to be some understanding of which of the listed variables has the greatest effect on an individual's likelihood to repeat illicit activity. As Helmus reminds us, there is not necessarily one route:

> Individuals radicalize through heterogeneous pathways, with life histories, group experiences, and motivations all affecting radicalized individuals in different ways. Consequently, not all factors are necessary conditions for radicalization. However, the literature and basic social-science research suggest that other features in the environment are necessary for the radicalization process. (Noricks et al., 2009, pp. 94, 96)

Prison is a disruptive experience that would certainly qualify as another "feature in the environment" that could alter an individual's life history and motivation. On one hand, time spent in the correctional system may provide the necessary course modification to reduce one's passion to change the system, diminish a personal or collective desire for revenge, or even provide motivation for peaceful dialogue. Alternatively, it could exacerbate alienation, trigger post-traumatic stress disorder, or stimulate a need for religious change by establishing a Caliphate—all factors that lead to radicalization according to Helmus.

Any of these reasons can be felt individually or collectively. The literature suggests that terrorists are quite rational in their decision making, despite the judgment that society has placed on the act of terrorism itself. Hoffman affirms, "all terrorist groups have one trait in common: they do not commit actions randomly or senselessly" (Hoffman, 2006, p. 173). Crenshaw asserts that "the outstanding common characteristic of terrorists is their normality" (Crenshaw, 1981, p. 390). McCauley adds that, "terrorism is not to be understood as pathology, and that terrorists emerge out of a normal psychology of emotional commitment to cause and comrades" (McCauley, 2002, p. 5). Despite society's intentions to dissuade a terrorist from his cause and comrades by convicting him of a crime and imprisoning him, he still may be inclined to proceed along "a long trajectory to terrorism, a trajectory in which the individual moves slowly toward an apocalyptic view of the world and a correspondingly extreme behavioral commitment" (McCauley, 2002, p. 15).

A five- to eight-year prison sentence for material support to terrorism may be a precursor to additional dangerous activity. Even if those convicted of terrorism-related crimes did not originally see themselves as terrorists, the prison experience may spawn additional grievances, facilitate new criminal contacts, or hone new skills to be put in the service of terrorism. Crenshaw's point resonates here: "If there is a single common emotion that drives the individual to become a terrorist, it is vengeance on behalf of comrades or even the constituency the terrorist aspires to represent" (Crenshaw, 1981, p. 394)

What considerations should be made to ensure they do not pose further risk? The individual and his "commitment to cause" are handled in different ways outside the United States. This is where the variance between the disciplines of social work and law enforcement are evident.

There is a wide range of approaches. In Singapore, the Religious Rehabilitation Group (RRG) is a group of religious scholars who aim through dialogue "to tackle the misunderstood aspects of Islam that are used to legitimize violence," (The FATA Secretariat Capacity Building Project, 2010) mainly by those former members of Jemaah Islamiyah (JI) (The FATA Secretariat Capacity Building Project, 2010, p. 8). The Indonesian counterterrorism unit, Detachment 88, engages detained terrorists about their ideologies and personal lives to leverage future cooperation upon release (Risk Reduction for Countering Violent Extremism, 2010, p. 21). The French government, however, "explicitly dismisses the potential value" (Risk Reduction for Countering Violent Extremism, 2010) of deradicalization and rehabilitation programs and relies on its intelligence, law enforcement and judiciary to fight Islamist extremism (Risk Reduction for Countering Violent Extremism, 2010, p. 42).

Stateside, Travis suggests that we ask the following question for every prisoner leaving American prisons:

> 'What will it take to keep this prisoner from committing another crime or being the victim of a crime?' In essence, we should create a safety plan for each prisoner to provide a safe transition over the first few months following release.... We would do everything we could to ensure a transition from prison that reduces the chances of rearrest and victimization, and enhances the chances of success. (J. Travis, 2006, pp. 114–115)

Can Travis's schema be extended to those associated with terrorism-related crimes, or any crimes with a national security nexus for that matter? Will the country look to rehabilitate this group of ex-convicts? How would such action be perceived? Prison ministries already exist to facilitate the transition of ex-convicts from incarceration to freedom. Travis furthers the concept by introducing a "Community Justice Corporation," which shifts justice from a governmental function to a community function, based on the premise that reintegration into the community is a societal goal (J. Travis, 2006, pp. 58–59).

But as Monowar Hossain Akhand, Deputy Secretary for the Ministry of Home Affairs in Bangladesh has stated, "There may be possible protests of civil societies or citizens who misunderstand the rehabilitation process as patronizing or supporting the criminals" (The International Conference on Terrorist Rehabilitation, 2009, p. 26). While terrorist therapy or integration may not be perceived as beneficial or generally welcomed by constituents, each is a preventive function that may be helpful upon the release from prison. The Risk Reduction Project stated that these efforts are:

> ...not just of "deradicalization" or "terrorist rehabilitation" programs, but also of strategic counter-terrorism approaches ... Reducing the risk of engagement (and/or re-engagement) in terrorism was the key and

singularly common feature across this array of programs. (Risk Reduction for Countering Violent Extremism, 2010, p. 1)

This could explain why some police departments in the United States have established Muslim outreach programs to facilitate open communication and strengthen trust. Kruglanski and Gelfand of the University of Maryland have been conducting research using psychological basics to examine the success of deradicalization processes (The International Conference on Terrorist Rehabilitation, 2009, p. 28). However, the American ability to deradicalize extremists is still questionable:

> While the U.S. and other Western countries can play a critical role in providing support in implementing and running 'deprogramming' counseling programs... a direct U.S. support may be counter-productive. It can provoke questions on the counselors' legitimacy and credibility. (The FATA Secretariat Capacity Building Project, 2010, p. 10)

Moreover, Travis adds that after prison, "the ex-felon is frequently reminded that his debt has not been paid as society continues to extract a price for violating its laws" (J. Travis, 2006, pp. 63–64). Post-prison injustices could aggravate existing grievances and stimulate motivations against the system that imprisoned him. In the absence of an adequate support network, someone who initially feels disenfranchised might be exponentially more vulnerable to radicalization and violence. He may join study groups focused on radical interpretations of Islam, and participate in internet discussion forums concentrating on violent jihad. Consequently, promotion of relevant arguments by the group may enable group extremity shift, eventually leading toward a terrorist attack (McCauley, 2002, p. 15).

Thus, in addition to examining efforts directed toward the individual, it is equally as important to gauge the environmental conditions to which a terrorist is exposed. Among the listed major imperatives for success defined by the Pakistani Federally Administered Tribal Areas (FATA) Capacity Building Project was:

> Rehabilitation and de-radicalization is a process that must be extended beyond the individual to include his family and community. Addressing ideological change in the individual without addressing his or her social

support network cannot ensure continuity of the process. (The FATA Secretariat Capacity Building Project, 2010, p. 28)

Helmus further stresses that, "(a)bundant evidence suggests that socialization processes are a necessary precondition for radicalization" (Noricks, Helmus, Paul, Berrebi, Jackson, Gvineria, Egner & Bahney, 2009, p. 96). Prison is a unique environment where socialization is required for survival. According to a prisoner radicalization task force report, "Inmates in general are particularly vulnerable to radical religious ideology due to their antisocial attitudes and the need to identify with other inmates sharing the same background, beliefs, or ethnicity" (Out of the Shadows: Getting Ahead of Prisoner Radicalization, 2006, p. 4). An inmate's choice of which group to join during prison, as well as a freed convict's choice of which group to join after prison will likely correlate to his propensity toward or away from future trouble.

Social identity theory asserts, "being categorized as members of certain groups provides an important part of the self-concept of individuals" (Brannan, Esler, & Strindberg, 2001, p. 17). Is being a prison inmate part of an individual's self-concept? What self-concept is prioritized in life after release from prison? Does an individual retain the same identity that he had before he was locked up (such as salesman, Muslim, gang member, sports fan, drug dealer)? Or does he identify with a new identity based on his prison experience (ex-con, extremist, student, criminal, born-again)? And to what extent does either identity remain with the individual following his release from prison? Shadd Maruna, a reader in criminology from Northern Ireland, argues:

> To desist from crime, ex-offenders need to develop a coherent, pro-social identity for themselves. As such, they need to account for and understand their criminal pasts... and they also need to understand why they are now 'not like that anymore.' Ex-offenders need a coherent and credible self-story to explain (to themselves and others) how their checkered pasts could have led to their new, reformed identities. (Maruna, 2001, pp. 7–8)

This is why the philosophies of popular deradicalization efforts center on the premise of deconstructing and reconstructing the social identity of those released from prison. This is done to distance terrorists from the groups that got them in trouble in the first place, and instill behaviors and actions aligned with societal norms (Brannan, Esler, & Strindberg, 2001, p. 17). One of the most popular programs, run by the Saudis, provides a halfway house to prepare newly released detainees for normal life (The International Conference on Terrorist Rehabilitation, 2009, p. 16). Care Rehabilitation Centers include group meals, art therapy, recreation and other leisure activity to "build teamwork but also encourage acceptance and develop notions of inclusion" (Boucek, 2008, p. 18). As part of its CONTEST counter-terrorism strategy, the United Kingdom has begun to use former prisoners to engage in a narrative that challenges the tenets of their former social identity and undermine the extremist ideology they originally believed. In each case, the goal of social identity modification is to reduce the attractiveness of terrorism and present any association with it as undesirable.

However, a societal approach may not be transferable, successful, or even popular in the United States. Dutch social scientist Geert Hofstede's cultural analysis, as cited by Brannan, Esler and Strindberg, characterizes the United States as an individualist culture that "emphasize(s) interpersonal competition, individual achievement, enterprise and innovativeness, and easy separation from kin and other groups..." (Brannan, Esler, & Strindberg, 2001, p. 17). These attributes conflict with the core of the rehabilitative programs that are used to counter violent extremists. The American proclivity to focus on the individual (i.e., "every man for himself") and libertarian values ("don't tread on me") fail to position a released terrorist in an environment where collective achievements can be honored, close ties with ingroup members can be established and maintained, and a disinclination to innovate or diverge from established ways can be upheld (Brannan, Esler, & Strindberg, 2001, p. 17). Release from prison and subsequent freedom may not be enough of a reward to dissuade future illicit activity. Rather, it is possible that a fulfilled prison sentence may be seen as a reward for maintaining discipline and essentially beating the system, and also can elevate the status of an individual among his minions. Examples from gangs and organized crime syndicates have demonstrated that prison time may merit a badge of honor more than impose a penalty against the imprisoned. Unlike sex offenders who are often shunned by society upon release from prison, these groups are likely to welcome an ex-convict to a community of comrades-in-arms.

The concept of a deradicalization program in the United States is also controversial, because it scratches the surface of mind control. Should the United States government invest resources in the business of changing the thoughts of its citizens, despite their criminal history, or is a terrorist mindset untenable? How would an instrument be created to reliably measure the level of extremism in an ex-convict's thoughts or propensity to act again? Would such an assessment be conducted like a parole-based hearing, or would it be more clinical? Would there be any recourse for false positives? Can the United States even touch the religious component associated with Islamist extremism? Can an individual even be fully deradicalized? Many questions similar to these were asked in a RAND monograph published in December 2010. The report's authors ask:

> ...the United States does not have a domestic counter-radicalization strategy, much less deradicalization programs.... can or should the United States adopt a domestic counter-radicalization or deradicalization approach at the national or local level?" (Rabasa et al., 2010, p. 190)

It is interesting that such a question is limited in its construction. The issue of radicalization, especially with religious extremists, stretches *beyond* national or local government. Deradicalization efforts in other countries have included the use of Muslim nongovernmental organizations (NGOs) in the United Kingdom, and local communities in the Netherlands (Rabasa et al., 2010, p. 192). FBI Supervisory Special Agent Brad Deardorff concurs:

> Both British and Dutch security services recognized nongovernment agencies and community leaders as important parts of their counter-radicalization strategies. It is exceptionally difficult to disrupt the radicalization process once an individual has committed to Islamist ideology. Credible voices are required to intervene with a religiously motivated recruit to terrorism. It is more likely that a radicalized subject would respond positively to someone who can speak with religious
>
> auhority and shares a common background than with a government agent who represents the "evil" that the subject might be radicalized against. (Deardorff, 2010, pp. 78–79)

The United States is not constrained to replicate efforts that are being used in other countries. However, it does need to understand what motivations are behind existing efforts. Some tactics may be unnecessary, some may lean up against the parameters set by national laws, and some may be outright illegal. Are the rules different for "at risk individuals" (those who have not yet committed a crime) than for ex-convicts (who have already completed prison time)? Can ex-convicts be forbidden from going to certain places, such as religious congregations led by inflammatory imams? How can the individual be isolated from hostile influences? Should military authorities and off-site facilities be leveraged to facilitate treatment until deradicalization has been completed? In what civics courses, community service endeavors, or other activities should he be immersed, in order to contribute to the betterment of society?

The tool kit used here may vary from what is used elsewhere. And the tension between effectiveness and social acceptance will likely be high in a country where political palatability is important. Is there a middle ground or are these outcomes mutually exclusive of each other? Alternatives within the proposals may be parsed in many ways into a menu of options that will take time for the American public to sort out and determine what is necessary to address this imminent reality.

It is important to determine what the goal of any policy is prior to introducing any new initiative, like that of an American deradicalization program. As David Tucker paraphrases Crenshaw, "depending on which approach or perspective we take, different counterterrorism responses (deterrence, appeasement, disruption) will appear to be more effective, while others will appear not to work at all or to even encourage more terrorism" (Tucker, 2009, p. 1). Each of these counterterrorism responses is designed to reduce risk; which measures best apply may vary because the rules for risk reduction may change when we deal with a set of individuals who have already been through the system.

This is a complex matter, which, like other homeland security issues, "will continually evolve in unpredictably interactive and uncontrollable ways. It is not obvious what decisions one can make today to affect outcomes in the complexity space (Bellavita, 2006, p. 6). The most important and logical first step is to identify who may impact or be impacted by any action taken in the complexity space where convicted and released terrorists reside, so we can begin a national discourse about it.

THIS PAGE INTENTIONALLY LEFT BLANK

VII. STRATEGY: IT TAKES A MEGACOMMUNITY

(T)he failure to put in place an effective long-term
counterterrorist strategy takes its place in the queue
of other short-term "fixes" that have had the effect
of delivering immediate results while arguably
undermining the prospects of long-term security.

– Hoffman, 2009, p. 361

The fact that this research about convicted and released terrorists produced zero evident ripples could be used to argue that existing "fixes," like prison sentences for example, are effective. If that were true, one might note that those fixes were not developed as part of a long-term strategy, but are rather ad hoc or coincidental. Part of the problem is certainly that even an issue as specific as the convicted and released terrorist is too large for one entity to assume responsibility over.

Four senior managers of the consulting firm Booz Allen Hamilton—Gerencser, Van Lee, Napolitano, and Kelly (hereafter, "Gerencser et al.")—introduced the notion of the "megacommunity" to address complex issues like this. The concept recognizes that there are "problems that no single organization (or methodology) can solve alone" (Gerencser et al., 2008, p. 18). More specifically:

> A megacommunity is a public sphere in which organizations from three sectors—business, government, and civil society—deliberately join together around compelling issues of mutual importance, following a set of practices and principles that make it easier for them to achieve results without sacrificing their individual goals.... a gathering place, not of individuals, but of organizations. (Gerencser et al., 2008, p. 53)

Elements of this model are applicable to the issue of convicted and released terrorists, regardless of their trajectory toward rehabilitation, moderation, or radicalization.

It would be presumptuous for the author of this research to both draw attention toward a new segment of literature, and unilaterally suggest the single method or one policy solution to address it. This research does not claim what 9/11 widow and author of *Because I Say So: The Dangers of Moral Authority* Nikki Stern calls the "moral authority" to propose what is right. Stern (2010) continues:

101

The world seems at times filled with people convinced beyond the shadow of a doubt they are uniquely qualified to know and represent what is right... (3) We tend less toward dialogue and more toward self-expression, and we seem more invested than ever in being right... we're still faced with the challenge of knowing what information to trust. (Stern, 2010, p. 10)

In essence, assuming such authority when the best plan has yet to be developed would limit the value of a final product. Even the authors of The 9/11 Commission Report, the first comprehensive narrative on terrorism in the United States, recognized "We are conscious of our limits.... New information inevitably will come to light (Kean et al., 2004, p. xvii). Heeding the advice of Singapore's minister of Foreign Affairs, George Yong-Boon Yeo, this author has chosen to "(a)dopt the attitude of a student and don't be too quick to preach.... If you think you are there to teach before you have learned, you will fail" (Gerencser et al., 2008, p. 91). Such a course of action is also proposed by Daniel Forrester in his 2011 book, *Consider*, who suggests that "taking time and giving ourselves the mental space for reflection can mean the difference between total success and total failure" (Forrester, n.d.).

Therefore, as we reflect upon the ten years that have passed since the largest terrorist attack in American history, it is incumbent upon the nation to recognize what is imminent in the next ten years and beyond. Despite the limited literature and data on the reentry of a convicted terrorist in America, it is inevitable that convicted terrorists will complete their prison sentences. The think tanks Proteus USA and Forecasting International acknowledge this phenomenon (Cetron & Davies, 2008).

Over the next decade or so, many of these prisoners will complete their terms and be paroled back into a society that offers them little future. Those who do not join terrorist cells out of belief could do so merely to gain a modest income. It is this idea, that potentially thousands of new jihadis, experienced with weapons and street combat and with little love for or stake in American society, could soon be out on the streets that so worries law enforcement officials. (Cetron & Davies, 2008, p. 7)

Thus, further scholarship is essential to learn more about the end of the terrorism continuum (post-event, post-conviction, post-prison, post-release). At this time, there is no distinct solution on how to address this issue, there is no single authority for convicted and released terrorists, and summarily, there is much more to learn about the subject than to prescribe. Thus, this thesis provides a prologue for scholars, practitioners, and policy makers from government, business, and civil society to consider when faced with decisions about the ripples caused by a convicted and released terrorist in America.

If learning among these associates is best achieved through broad community engagement, we can begin by focusing on what is required to generate awareness about what we have discussed and expand upon what we know. Awareness may range from a vague sense of public knowledge to participation and action in specific projects or institutional settings. Where a new strategy may begin with general education among opinion makers, it may very well lead to the creation of a collaborative network with different stakeholders with vested interests in program management (Bach, 2010). It is more than a formal organizational public relations campaign. As Gerencser et al. emphasize:

> Megacommunity thinking not only requires that individuals use and develop their own awareness. They must be prepared to build awareness across the megacommunity—an awareness that reflects not only the founding mission, goals, terms, and conditions of engagement, but also an awareness of how to handle what might be in the megacommunity's future. (Gerencser et al., 2008, p. 96)

This is our starting point, as the implications drawn from this research provide something tangible from which to begin the discourse. The quantitative significance is less important than the concepts, problems, and processes that are extracted from the affected groups.

Any strategy is likely to evolve depending upon the ripples caused by convicted terrorists after their release from prison. It is not necessarily important to know what specific outcome will be favored at this point in the sequence. The greater challenge, rather, is to create a dialogue that explores the profundity of this phenomenon based on further analysis, academic debate, and general public interest to test what options are viable and construct propositions that determine how answers are socially constructed.

One of our findings stated that there is no defined entity responsible for examining convicted terrorists following their term of supervised release. Upon

103

reflection, the declaration of one party for such a responsibility actually would be irresponsible right now. If we were to conclude our work by tasking a national or local JTTF to monitor the issue, we would inevitably produce bias toward a law enforcement solution. If we independently prescribed deradicalization assessments to support the efforts of the social science community, our solution will also be partial at best. Shortcomings would even exist if we were to designate what we thought was a "complete" set of organizations that should influence the narrative. Though the outset of this research was centered on a defined subject, stimulation of interest is critical to arouse any sense of accountability or ownership. Gerencser et al. state:

> Megacommunity leadership is not a prescriptive kind of the strategy (that is, prescribing the details that others have to perform). The successful megacommunity leader is one who stimulates the need to collaborate, invents strategies that work for everybody, and keeps people motivated along those lines. (Gerencser et al., 2008, pp. 199–200)

There can be accountability, but not necessarily in the role of the traditional manager. Rather, a catalyst is necessary to integrate multiple organizations and tackle large issues. According to Gerencser et al.:

> While the potential energy is there, the creation of a megacommunity requires a catalyst to convert the potential energy into action. Allowing for the fact that in a moment of crisis—such as a natural disaster—a megacommunity might spontaneously emerge, in most cases, an initiator, or group of initiators, will have to step forward. (Gerencser et al., 2008, p. 113)

In *The Starfish and The Spider*, Brafman and Beckstrom further purport that catalysts hold the responsibility of settling disputes and mapping direction among groups, interests, and ideas toward some set of potential outcomes (Brafman & Beckstrom, 2006, pp. 109–120). While prospective options may appear evident at the start of the process, it is best to be prepared to accept that the final outcome may mutate from the structure that is originally established. For example, federal authorities will initially have different perspectives on convicted and released terrorists than local ones. It is likely that the American Civil Liberties Union (ACLU) will contrast some views of the Intelligence and National Security Alliance (INSA). Ultimately, the catalyst "can help get the megacommunity off the ground" through existing relationships with multiple organizations, provide stakeholder groups with some semblance of organization, stimulate a narrative and produce a strategy with execution built into its core (Gerencser et al., 2008, p. 121).

Such a multidimensional approach is not new to the field of homeland security; rather it is becoming the norm. In fact, the subject of handling convicted and released terrorists could serve as a microcosm for the many coordination challenges faced by the Department of Homeland Security on a daily basis.

But even DHS in its coordination mission cannot and should not be solely responsible for this effort, nor should existing organizations, such as the International Association of Chiefs of Police (IACP), the FBI's InfraGard Program, the American Psychological Association (APA), INSA, or the ACLU, to name a handful. The subject of convicted and released terrorists may be worth exploring with analytical rigor by an interdisciplinary fusion center, but even then, there are influences propagated by the funding recipient responsible for managing the unit.

Our decision to identify the multiple disciplines that interact with our target of study helped us better understand those stakeholders with interrelated responsibilities in the homeland security network, and enabled us to assess the existence of collaboration directed toward our niche population. But more importantly, this process informed us that the ordered structure of the system introduces more questions than easily resolvable solutions for the population of convicted and released terrorists. According to Bellavita:

> The issues in this domain are "open problems." They are *open* because they will never go away or be resolved fully. They are *problems* in both a functional sense (they are a source of grief and opportunity) and in a philosophical sense (they are issues from which the future of homeland security will emerge). *The planning methodologies and strategic tools that work well in the ordered domain of known and knowable issues are ineffective in the domain of the unordered.* New modes of inquiry and action are needed if policymakers are to do more than watch the future of homeland security happen. (Emphasis added) (Bellavita, 2006, p. 8)

These new modes of inquiry and action can be well developed by a megacommunity of organizations who have no problem "playing in the mud" (Freier,

105

2009, pp. 25–26). This technique, envisioned for the Department of Defense, is described by Freier as an operating environment in which success is measured by the ability to: navigate through organizational dysfunction, educate through cultural ignorance, adapt to changed or changing conditions in the absence of operational clarity, accept risk as a constant, see the art of the possible through inherently muddy conditions, and be competitive against the adversary, not organizationally (Kiernan, 2010). Gerencser et al. add that megacommunity

> …participants remain interdependent because their common interest compels them to work together, even though they might not see, describe, or approach their mutual problem or situation in the same way…. Megacommunity protocols and principles create and maintain a *dynamic tension* between businesses, governments, and civil society as they attempt to operate simultaneously in the same space. (Gerencser et al., 2008, pp. 54, 56)

Members from all sectors should seek to define how associations are connected and ask the hard questions. Should the contacts of an ex-convict get forwarded from a federal prosecutor to a local police officer? What transitioning should occur between prison officials and family members? How does the role of religion affect policy between a convicted terrorist, the U.S. Attorney's Office, and the U.S. Courts? Do employers have a social responsibility to reintegrate convicted criminals, let alone terrorists, into society? How do sentencing guidelines for terrorism related crimes affect the general public? Does the absence of ripple effects serve an indicator of success, or cause reason for concern?

This is just a start. But, "All these questions get answered over time, as you steep yourself in systems thinking, and as you apply your own reflective ability to the results of the megacommunity's experiments" (Gerencser et al., 2008, p. 209). Members of this megacommunity should understand the roles of everyone else, and be prepared for conflict. In fact, "No one should be looking to eliminate conflict…. The problem exists, in part, because conflicts exist" (Gerencser et al., 2008, p. 157).

The International Conference on Terrorist Rehabilitation in Singapore and the Qatar International Academy for Security Studies Countering Violent Extremism Risk Reduction Project are examples of how complex issues that transcend organizational and national boundaries can be addressed. Each has "an eye toward the connections between local and global issues" (Gerencser et al., 2008, p. 139) across sectors. Foreign governments, religious organizations, academia, and private businesses each respectfully contribute to a global effort of magnanimous importance through varying lenses to learn from each other and "to reach the goals they cannot achieve alone" (Gerencser et al., 2008, p. 28).

Similar efforts could be initiated among affected stakeholders in the United States. Even though we do not know what ripples are created after a convicted terrorist is released from prison, we can begin to map out what network exists. Gerencser et al. say "the earliest stakeholder analysis… should result in the identification of hubs" (Gerencser et al., 2008, p. 138). Our initial research showed that the Federal Bureau of Prisons and probation officers of the U.S. Courts may serve as initial hubs for information. But if we were successful in identifying the locations of these individuals, local law enforcement would also clearly be recognized as a hub. Representatives from civil society (such as social work agencies) and the business sector (prospective employers) who work with convicted terrorists serve as additional nodes that connect into these respective hubs. Recognition of what hubs play important roles can help determine what additional links are needed to support relationships between communities. Instead of asking who is *responsible*, a more suitable question to ask is who is *connected*. Gerencser et al. inform us that "(m)egacommunity involvement teaches you to respect the value of the network and allows you to optimize that value" (Gerencser et al., 2008, p. 217). This is essential because the network is bigger than any one entity.

Concerns about convicted and released terrorists have not yet manifested themselves, but elevating visibility of the issue can reduce the unpredictability of the subject. By developing a community of organizations with a shared interest, society may be able to address issues proactively before they escalate, as well as disrupt any inertia or complacency that may exist. Before doing so, it will be necessary to create a common baseline of knowledge upon which future discourse can be built, based on terminology and values.

This topic is a springboard for many discussions that may require establishing some baseline level of agreement. Questions include, what is a terrorist? What is the appropriate balance between transparency and information protection? Is there a place for preemption in public policy? What are society's goals for the convicted terrorist after prison? There are no simple answers, but consensus may be reached through dialogue within a megacommunity. This values discussion has become even more pertinent in our increasingly globalized society and economy. Says Moghaddam:

> When we deal with a global system, how do we decide which justice system to go with? One set of people believes in cutting off the left hand. Another set of people think fifteen years of jail is the right way to go. Are there universal values that can be applied to determining what is justice? (F. Moghaddam, personal communication, January 4, 2011)

As we look to defining justice and punishment, Lang (2010) suggests that debate, rather than the introduction of new law, is required to address terrorists:

> Despite the myth that the legal process alone can solve these problems, it will not. Rather, such cases—indeed, any legal process—require more sustained political effort.... Until the international political community attends to the problems of terrorism and punishment through a *public deliberative process that includes a wide range of actors in the international community*, a mere turn to either national or international courts will not resolve these issues. A new values consensus is necessary, one that will emerge only through political debate. (Emphasis added) (Lang, 2010).

This values consensus is not solely a governmental decision. It is human, and it is societal. The law should not be underemphasized, however, as the courts will inevitably be engaged. As Alexis de Tocqueville wrote in his famous *Democracy in America* centuries ago, "there is hardly a political question in the United States, which does not sooner or later turn into a judicial one" (de Tocqueville, 1988).

The diversity of perspectives, missions, and interests that is intertwined within the political debate must be seen as a core strength of the megacommunity, not a liability. If its purpose is to achieve something that cannot be done by one organization, members must embrace transparency while maintaining their independence. Social scientists do not need to impede the work of the law enforcement agencies, and religious organizations do not need representation from civil libertarians. In other words:

> Megacommunity thinking does not seek to throw open or tear apart the functioning of any single organization…. megacommunity members should strive for complete transparency, regarding the aims of the megacommunity, their part in it, and their understanding of other players in the megacommunity. (Gerencser et al., 2008, p. 101)

Such an approach is consistent with how members of the intelligence community are beginning to conduct their affairs. In his message prefacing the 2008 Intelligence Community Information Sharing Strategy, Director of National Intelligence Mike McConnell said "Together, we must challenge the status quo of a 'need-to-know' culture and move to one of a 'responsibility to provide' mindset" (United States Intelligence Community Information Sharing Strategy, 2008). The same point could be made for a megacommunity examining convicted and released terrorists. Can some aspects of the 'responsibility to provide' stretch beyond the IC into the public domain? Yes. Can the group of participating organizations be too large, or can a list be too long? No, especially on a topic receiving little, if any attention to date like ours. The increase of information can help to steer the direction of the narrative. Says Gerencser et al., "a potential new member should not have to prove they belong in a specific megacommunity. Benefit of the doubt goes to the joiner" (Gerencser et al., 2008, p. 185).

Just as "layers of security" are applied to disrupt acts of terrorism against critical infrastructure, a layered approach can also help deter a convicted terrorist from reconnecting with his past. More importantly, the effort requires communication between those layers to be effective. That communication provides the glue for the megacommunity members to address its differing and overlapping interests.

Initially, communities must be built. As DHS Secretary Janet Napolitano urged in September 2009, "we should measure our nation's security not just by the borders we strengthen and the laws we enforce, but also by the strength and resilience of the communities we build" (Napolitano Stresses Shared Responsibility, 2009). The term "communities" should not be limited to geographic neighborhoods; it should include professional disciplines.

For example, the law enforcement community has more to accomplish in order to achieve national resilience. As former New York City Mayor Rudy Giuliani eulogized Jack Maple in 2002, he reflected upon one of the former NYPD deputy commissioner's frequent maxims: "The biggest lie in law enforcement is, 'We work well together.'" (Daly, 2002). The absence of an integrated domestic intelligence network that horizontally connects police departments to, for example, track convicted and released terrorists for potential recidivism does not exist (G. Rodriguez, personal communication, May 15, 2010). However, as American prisons house and release more convicted terrorists, such a community—beyond existing memoranda of understanding (MOUs) and task forces—will be essential to continuously deter homegrown terrorism in the United States.

Once communities are built, communities subsequently must connect. As Secretary Napolitano stated a year later, she "said her department wants to continue to build relationships with police." (Napolitano Warns Police Chiefs of Homegrown Threat, 2010). The same relationship building can be suggested between DHS and prisons, attorneys, social workers, academics, businesses, non-governmental organizations, as well as their international compatriots. As these bonds form, the narrative can evolve to better understand and address the critical imperatives of the future. It could be argued that the radicalization issue has yet to be "solved" because most of the burden rests with government. One sector, however, cannot address such complexity alone and requires what Gerencser et al. call, "convergence:"

> Convergence will occur when each separate constituency affected by any issue realizes that its progression has achieved a plateau or roadblock, when any additional effort does not produce further improvement. (Gerencser et al., 2008, p. 70)

There is evidence that the homeland security narrative is evolving toward convergence, nonetheless. The passage of time and tri-sector engagement between government, business, and civil society is beginning to enable such a shift to emerge. A *Time* magazine article in 2002 headlined "Do Good Neighbors Make Good Spies?" asked if "local vigilance (had) gone overboard" after the Portland Seven (which includes two members of our dataset) were turned in for suspicious activity by members of the local community (Ripley, Forster & Thornburgh, 2002). Yet nearly a decade later, not only is citizen action deemed laudable, but the President of the United States has positively recognized the watchful eyes of the Times Square vendor who disrupted Faisal Shahzad's car bomb attempt (Gendar, 2010), and the New York Metropolitan Transit Authority's trademarked "See Something, Say Something" slogan has been hotly pursued by DHS along with "transit authorities in Boston, Chicago, Amsterdam and about 50 other locations" (Feds to Riders: "See Something, Say Something," 2010). The "See Something, Say Something" message has come to signify something more than a governmental catchphrase; it also now represents an American responsibility for government, civil society, and business, as neither can operate in a vacuum. This narrative continues to endure through "permanent negotiation," which:

> ...defines a state of constant interaction and exchange between the members of the megacommunity. It calls for individuals to recognize the need for constant stakeholder engagement. (Gerencser et al., 2008, p. 100)

The megacommunity is the appropriate forum through which the narrative can evolve, as long as participants are able to recognize "a well-developed 'overlapping vital interest' (that) suggests potential actions that can be taken" (Gerencser et al., 2008, p. 140). Here, so long as a vital interest remains in convicted terrorists who are released from prison, so should the megacommunity.

While we do not have expectations for what will be identified or how such information will be measured or defined, the extensive considerations that are created by the reemergence of a terrorist in American society merit examination, as we may face a serious issue that threatens our freedom, hidden in plain sight.

THIS PAGE INTENTIONALLY LEFT BLANK

LIST OF REFERENCES

The ACLU of Nevada wins temporary stay of new sex offender laws. (2008, July 18). Retrieved October 28, 2010, from http://www.aclunv.org/aclu-nevada-wins-temporary-stay-new-sex-offender-laws

Acts of terrorism transcending national boundaries, 18U.S.C. U.S. Code, Pt. I. 2010 ed., Ch. 113B, § 2332b Retrieved December 7, 2010, from http://www.law.cornell.edu/uscode/html/uscode18/usc_sec_18_00002332---b000-.html#g_5_B

Administration transfers 12 Gitmo detainees overseas, despite concerns. (2009). Retrieved December 20, 2009, from http://www.foxnews.com/politics/2009/12/20/administration-transfers-gitmo-detainees-overseas-despite-concerns/

Albrecht, H. J., & Kilchling, M. (2007). Victims of terrorism policies: Should victims of terrorism be treated differently? *European Journal on Criminal Policy & Research, 13*(1/2), 13-31. doi:10.1007/s10610-007-9038-3.

America's unjust sex laws. (2009, August 6). Retrieved November 12, 2010, from http://www.economist.com/node/14165460?story_id=14165460

Bach, R. (2010, October 7). In Brown M. (Ed.), *Strategic planning and budgeting for homeland security*. Monterey, California: Naval Postgraduate School, Center for Homeland Defense and Security.

Barnes, J. E., & Parsons, C. (2010, January 7). *More former Guantánamo detainees returning to militant activity, Pentagon says.* Retrieved March 28, 2010, from http://articles.latimes.com/2010/jan/07/nation/la-na-Guantánamo-repeaters7-2010jan07

Barnes, R. (2010, May 18, 2010). 'Sexually dangerous' inmates can be held indefinitely, Supreme Court rules. *Washington Post*, p. A6. Retrieved May 18, 2010 from http://www.washingtonpost.com/wp-dyn/content/article/2010/05/17/AR2010051703593_pf.html

BBC News. (2010). *Bail-jumping Basque de Juana appeals extradition.* Retrieved May 15, 2010, from http://news.bbc.co.uk/2/hi/uk_news/northern_ireland/8682957.stm

Bell, S. (2007, August 31). 'Vigilant eye' on returning terrorist: Day; Canadian Accused Of Conspiring With Hamas Released. *National Post (f/k/a the Financial Post) (Canada)*, p. A5.

Bellavita, C. (2006, October). Changing homeland security: Shape patterns, not programs. *Homeland Security Affairs, II*(3), Retrieved January 18, 2010, from http://www.hsaj.org/?fullarticle=2.3.5

Bergen, P., & Hoffman, B. (2010, September 10). *Assessing the terrorist threat: A Report of the bipartisan policy center's national security preparedness group.* Retrieved September 15, 2010, from http://bipartisanpolicy.org/sites/default/files/NSPG%20Final%20Threat%20Assessment.pdf

Bjelopera, J. P., & Randol, M. A. (2010, December 7). *American jihadist terrorism: Combating a complex threat.* Washington, D.C.: Congressional Research Service. No. R41416. Retrieved December 19, 2010, from http://www.fas.org/sgp/crs/terror/R41416.pdf.

Bonin, R. (Producer) (2010, April 25). *The narrative. 60 minutes.* [Motion Picture] United States: Columbia Broadcasting System. Retrieved April 25, 2010, from http://www.cbsnews.com/video/watch/?id=6430933n

BOP: Inmate locator main page. (n.d.). Retrieved May 5, 2010, from http://www.bop.gov/iloc2/LocateInmate.jsp

Boucek, C. (2008). *Saudi Arabia's "soft" counterterrorism strategy: Prevention, rehabilitation, and aftercare.* Washington, D.C.: Carnegie Endowment for International Peace. No. 97. Retrieved December 5, 2009, from http://www.carnegieendowment.org/files/cp97_boucek_saudi_final.pdf

Brafman, O., & Beckstrom, R. A. (2006). *The starfish and the spider.* New York: Penguin.

Brannan, D. W., Esler, P. F., & Strindberg, N. T. A. (2001). Talking to "terrorists:" Towards an independent analytical framework for the study of violent substate activism. *Studies in Conflict & Terrorism, 24*(1), 3–24. doi:10.1080/10576100118602

Bush, G. W. (2004, January 20). *Address before a joint session of the Congress on the state of the union.* Retrieved October 16, 2010, from http://www.c-span.org/executive/transcript.asp?cat=current_event&code=bush_admin&year=2004

Cannon, W. R. (2009, October 17). Preventing the next generation of terrorists: Probation and supervision of detainees after their release. Message posted to https://www.chds.us/courses/mod/forum/discuss.php?d=25587#p81015

Cetron, M. J., & Davies, O. (2008). *55 trends now shaping the future of terrorism.* Retrieved March 31, 2010, from http://www.au.af.mil/au/awc/awcgate/army/proteus-55-terror.pdf

Charivari. (n.d.). Retrieved December 5, 2009, from http://www.faqs.org/childhood/Bo-Ch/Charivari.html

Cohen, A. (2009). *Gitmo fate mired in fuzzy math.* Retrieved December 8, 2009, from http://www.cbsnews.com/stories/2009/01/26/opinion/courtwatch/main4753392.shtml

Connecticut's sex offender website registry violates rights, court rules. (2001). Retrieved October 28, 2010, from http://www.aclu.org/racial-justice_drug-law-reform_immigrants-rights_womens-rights/connecticuts-sex-offender-website-reg

Convicted terrorists should be watched upon release—Russian defence minister. (2005, January 11). *BBC Monitoring Former Soviet Union—Political Supplied by BBC Worldwide Monitoring.*

Court bails ETA extradition man. (2008, November 18). Retrieved December 5, 2009, from http://news.bbc.co.uk/2/hi/uk_news/northern_ireland/7733126.stm

Crabtree, S. (2010, March 26). *Justice Department gives Republicans requested info on terrorism convictions.* Retrieved April 3, 2010, from http://thehill.com/homenews/house/89347-gop-gets-requested-info-on-terrorism-convictions?sms_ss=delicious

Crenshaw, M. (1981, July). The causes of terrorism. *Comparative Politics, 13*(4), 379–399.

Crenshaw, M. (2007). The debate over "new" vs. "old" terrorism. Paper presented at the *Annual Meeting of the American Political Science Association,* Chicago, Illinois.

Cronin, A. K. (2006, Summer). How Al-Qaida ends. *International Security, 21*(1), 7–48.

Cronin, A. K., Preble, C. A., Sageman, M., & Mack, A. (2009). Panel III: Terrorist groups: A status report. Paper presented at the *Cato Institute's Two Day Conference: Shaping the Obama Administration's Counterterrorism Strategy,* Washington, D.C. Retrieved April 9, 2010, from http://www.cato.org/events/counterterrorism/index.html

Daly, M. (2002, February 13). *Cop putting heat on FBI over secrecy.* Retrieved December 8, 2010, from http://www.nydailynews.com/archives/news/2002/02/13/2002-02-13_cop_putting_heat_on_fbi_over.html

Davis, J. (2010). *Convicted terrorists living next door, deadly terror plot devised inside California prison.* Retrieved January 31, 2010, from http://www.examiner.com/x-35807-LA-Homeland-Security-Examiner~y2010m1d28-Convicted-terrorists-living-next-door-deadly-terror-plot-devised-inside-California-prison?cid=exrss-LA-Homeland-Security-Examiner

Davis, P. K., & Jenkins, B. M. (2002). *Deterrence & influence in counterterrorism: A component in the war on al Qaeda.* Santa Monica, California: RAND National Defense Research Institute. Retrieved September 13, 2009, from http://www.rand.org/content/dam/rand/pubs/monograph_reports/2005/MR1619.pdf

de Tocqueville, A. (1988, September). In Mayer J. P. (Ed.), *Democracy in America.* New York, NY: Harper Perennial.

Deardorff, R. B. (2010, December). *Countering violent extremism: The challenge and the opportunity.* (M.A., Naval Postgraduate School). Retrieved January 29, 2011, from http://edocs.nps.edu/npspubs/scholarly/theses/2010/Dec/10Dec_Deardorff.pdf

DHS releases 5 terrorists into U.S. to test national security. (2010, August 5). *The Onion,* pp. 1, 4.

DoD news briefing with Geoff Morrell from the Pentagon. (2009, January 13). Retrieved December 8, 2009, from http://www.defense.gov/transcripts/transcript.aspx?transcriptid=4340

Dooghan, J. K. (2006). *Muslim prison ministry: Hindering the spread of the radical, militant, violent and irreconcilable wing of Islam.* Fort Leavenworth, Kansas: School of Advanced Military Studies, United States Army Command and General Staff College. Retrieved December 5, 2009, from http://handle.dtic.mil/100.2/ADA450078

Duties of Bureau of Prisons. 18 U.S.C. § 4042 (b) and (c). Retrieved July 16, 2010, from http://codes.lp.findlaw.com/uscode/18/III/303/4042

Eggen, D. (2006, November 30). U.S. Settles Suit Filed by Ore. Lawyer. Retrieved March 28, 2010, from http://www.washingtonpost.com/wp-dyn/content/article/2006/11/29/AR2006112901179.html

Emerson, S. (2002). *American jihad: The terrorists living among us.* New York, NY: Free Press.

ETA terrorist Iñaki De Juana Chaos released from prison after 21 years. (2008, August 4). Retrieved December 4, 2009, from http://www.surinenglish.com/20080802/news/spain/de_juana_chaos-200808021010.html

Eviatar, D. (2009, November 25). *Can the death penalty for terrorists fuel violence?* Retrieved March 27, 2010, from http://washingtonindependent.com/68913/can-the-death-penalty-for-terrorists-fuel-violence

Executive session—prisoner reentry, Oct. 7. (n.d.). Retrieved October 27, 2010, from http://www.policeforum.org/news/detail.dot?id=45983

116

The FATA Secretariat Capacity Building Project. (2010, May 18–19). *1st strategic workshop on rehabilitation and de-radicalization of militants and extremists.* Report on a Workshop Organized by S. Rajaratnam School of International Studies: Singapore.

FBI—Community outreach. (n.d.). Retrieved September 3, 2010, from http://www.fbi.gov/hq/ood/opca/outreach/copintro.htm

FBI—What we investigate. (n.d.). Retrieved August 30, 2010, from http://www.fbi.gov/hq.htm

Federal court sides with ACLU in sex offender consent-to-search case. (2008, June 24). Retrieved October 28, 2010, from http://www.courierpress.com/news/2008/jun/24/24WEB-sexoffenderlawsuit/

Feds to riders: "See something, say something." (2010, July 1). Retrieved December 5, 2010, from http://www.cbsnews.com/stories/2010/07/01/national/main6637619.shtml

Felleman, H. (Ed.). (1936). *Best loved poems of the American people.* New York, NY: Doubleday.

Fink, N. C., & Hearne, E. B. (2008, October). *Beyond terrorism: Deradicalization and disengagement from violent extremism.* New York: International Peace Institute. Retrieved January 18, 2011, from http://www.humansecuritygateway.com/documents/IPA_BeyondTerrorism.pdf

Finn, P., & Kornblut, A. E. (2010, December 22). Indefinite detention possible for suspects at Guantánamo Bay. *Washington Post,* p. A03. Retrieved December 22, 2010, from http://www.washingtonpost.com/wp-dyn/content/article/2010/12/21/AR2010122105523.html

Forbes, M., & Coorey, P. (2007, October 12). Victims' families outraged that Bali bombers attended party. *Sydney Morning Herald (Australia),* p. 7.

Forrester, D. P. (n.d.). *The book | upon reflection.* Retrieved January 21, 2011, from http://danielforrester.com/?page_id=36

Fox, B. (2009, October 15). *Reported plea deal in Guantánamo case draws fire.* Retrieved October 16, 2010, from http://news.yahoo.com/s/ap/20101015/ap_on_re_la_am_ca/cb_Guantánamo_war_crimes_1

Franklin, B., & Franklin, W. T. (Eds.). (1818). *Memoirs of the life and writings of Benjamin Franklin.* London: A. J. Valpy. Retrieved November 13, 2010, from http://books.google.com/books?id=W2MFAAAAQAAJ&pg=PA270&lpg=PA270t#v=onepage&q&f=false

Freier, N. (2009, June). *DoD leaders, strategists, and operators in an era of persistent unconventional challenge.* Washington, D.C.: Center for Strategic & International Studies.

Gendar, A. (2010, October 6). *Street vendor Duane Jackson, who alerted cops to Faisal Shahzad bomb threat, is taking FBI classes.* Retrieved December 5, 2010, from http://www.nydailynews.com/ny_local/2010/10/06/2010-10-06_undaunted_hero_still_at_his_post_on_w_45th.html

Gerencser, M., Van Lee, R., Napolitano, F., & Kelly, C. (2008). *Megacommunities: How leaders of government, business, and non-profits can tackle today's global challenges together.* New York: Palgrave Macmillan.

Gerstein, J. (2010). *Obama revives terror-prison rules.* Retrieved April 7, 2010, from http://dyn.politico.com/printstory.cfm?uuid=D59155F7-18FE-70B2-A8D877E272290364

Glaser, B. G., & Strauss, A. L. (1967). *The discovery of grounded theory.* New York: Aldine De Gruyter.

Goldby, B. (2009, October 25). Behead terror gang are freed; Conspirators serve less than two years: exclusive. *Sunday Mercury*, p. 7.

Guantánamo suicides 'acts of war'. (2006, June 11). Retrieved March 28, 2010, from http://news.bbc.co.uk/2/hi/5068606.stm

Hayden, M. (2010, October 29). *Criminal law, national security and the First Amendment.* Freedom Forum, First Amendment Center, Newseum. Washington, D.C.: C-SPAN Video Library.

The Herald Square Plot: A NEFA analysis of U.S. v. Siraj. (2008, March). No. Report #14 in a NEFA series, "Target: America." The NEFA Foundation. Retrieved August 24, 2010, from http://www.nefafoundation.org/miscellaneous/FeaturedDocs/HeraldSquarePlot.pdf

Hesterman, J. (2010, May 21). *Who is Khalid Ouazzani?* Retrieved May 24, 2010, from http://jennihesterman.blogspot.com/2010/05/who-is-khalid-ouazzani.html

Hickley, M. (2008, March 31). Straw 'con trick' over early-release terrorists. *Daily Mail (London)*, p. 8.

Hicks to be watched. (2007, April 9). *The Australian (Australia),* p. 2.

Higgins, E. (2009, April 6). Moderates to help in fighting terror. *The Australian,* p. 6.

'High risk' convicted terrorists live in bail hostels in Britain. (2009, July 19). Retrieved February 3, 2010, from www.thaindian.com/newsportal/world-news/high-risk-convicted-terrorists-live-in-bail-hostels-in-britain_100220001.html

Hoffman, B. (2006). *Inside terrorism.* New York, NY: Columbia University Press.

Hoffman, B. (2009). A counterterrorism strategy for the Obama administration. *Terrorism and Political Violence, 21*(3), 359–377. doi:10.1080/09546550902950316

Hoffman, B., & Kasupski, A. (2007). *Victims of terrorism: An assessment of their influence & growing role in policy, legislation & the private sector.* Santa Monica, CA: RAND Center for Terrorism Risk Management Policy.

How many detainees go back to terrorism? (2009, May 21). Retrieved March 28, 2010, from http://ac360.blogs.cnn.com/2009/05/21/how-many-detainees-go-back-to-terrorism/

Human Factors/Behavioral Sciences Division. Science and Technology Directorate. U.S. Department of Homeland Security University of Maryland: National Consortium for the Study of Terrorism and Responses to Terrorism. (2010, February 16). *Community-level indicators of radicalization: A data and methods task force.* Report. Retrieved November 12, 2010, from http://www.start.umd.edu/start/publications/START_HFD_CommRadReport.pdf

Hurtado, P. (2010, October 29). *Ex-terrorist Meskini gets 31 months more in prison.* Retrieved October 30, 2010, from http://www.businessweek.com/news/2010-10-29/ex-terrorist-meskini-gets-31-months-more-in-prison.html

Hurtado, P., & Kary, T. (2010). *Afzali avoids prison for lying about New York subway bomb plot.* Retrieved April 16, 2010, from http://www.bloomberg.com/apps/news?pid=20670001&sid=amrxOr_5KYcI

Inbari, P. (2010, January 4). The Barghouti dilemma. *The Jerusalem Report*, p. 15.

Indonesia says no more remissions, pardons for terror offenders. (2010, March 16). *BBC Monitoring Asia Pacific—Political Supplied by BBC Worldwide Monitoring, InfraGard—Public private partnership—Federal Bureau of Investigation.* (n.d.). Retrieved September 3, 2010, from http://www.infragard.net/

The International Conference on Terrorist Rehabilitation. (2009). Paper presented at the *The International Conference on Terrorist Rehabilitation,* S. Rajaratnam School of International Studies, Nanyang Technological University, Singapore. Retrieved December 5, 2009, from http://www.pvtr.org/pdf/Report/RSIS_ICTR_Report_2009.pdf

Ismail, N. H. (2010). *Prison radicalization and how it happens: An analysis into root causes of terrorism.* Retrieved August 27, 2010, from http://www.thejakartapost.com/news/2010/08/27/prison-radicalization-and-how-it-happens-an-analysis-root-causes-terrorism.html

Jacobson, M. (2010). *Terrorist dropouts: Learning from those who have left.* The Washington Institute for Near East Policy.

Janus, E. S. (2004). *The preventive state, terrorists and sexual predators: Countering the threat of a new outsider jurisprudence.* Retrieved August 23, 2010, from http://www.blueshifthome.com/misc/40%20Crim%20L%20Bull%20576%20-%202004.pdf

Jenkins, B. M. (2010). *Would-be warriors: incidents of jihadist terrorist radicalization in the United States since September 11, 2001.* Retrieved July 18, 2010, from http://www.rand.org/pubs/occasional_papers/2010/RAND_OP292.pdf

Jimenez, M. (2009, September 28) (1998, November 7, Reprint). *From the archives: Hijacker fears torture, death if deported from Canada.* Retrieved February 3, 2010, from http://www.nationalpost.com/related/topics/story.html?id=2043874

Johnson, C. (2009, March 18). *Prison officials are loosening restrictions on Taliban supporter.* Retrieved September 22, 2010, from http://www.washingtonpost.com/wp-dyn/content/article/2009/03/17/AR2009031702356.html

Johnston, P. (2008, March 29). Terrorists freed early in scheme to ease jail crowding. *The Daily Telegraph (LONDON),* p. 9.

Kaminer, W. (2010, May 20). *When the Feds decide who's sexually dangerous.* Retrieved October 27, 2010, from http://www.theatlantic.com/national/archive/2010/05/when-the-feds-decide-whos-sexually-dangerous/57005/

Kean, T. H., Hamilton, L. H., Ben-Veniste, R., Kerrey, B., Fielding, F. F., Lehman, J. F., . . . Gorton, S., & Thompson, J. R. (2004). *The 9/11 commission report: Final report of the National Commission on terrorist attacks upon the United States.* New York: W.W. Norton & Company.

Kean: Abdulmutallab 'did us a favor'. (2010, January 3). Retrieved March 27, 2010, from http://www.politico.com/blogs/politicolive/0110/Kean_Obama_Was_Not_Focused_on_Terrorism.html

Kennedy, D. (2009, June 9). *The myth of Guantánamo recidivism.* Retrieved March 28, 2010, from http://www.guardian.co.uk/commentisfree/cifamerica/2009/jun/09/Guantánamo-new-york-times

Khatarish, A., Al-Qarni, I. & Al-Jura, Q. (2009). *Life after prison: Roadblocks to social re-entry.* Retrieved December 4, 2009, from http://www.saudigazette.com.sa/index.cfm?method=home.regcon&contentID=2008102420044

Kiernan, K. (2010, June 29). *Inter-disciplinary approaches to homeland security.* Monterey, California: Naval Postgraduate School, Center for Homeland Defense and Security.

Koch, W. (2006, June 6). *More sex offenders tracked by satellite.* Retrieved November 4, 2010, from http://www.usatoday.com/tech/news/techinnovations/2006-06-06-gps-tracking_x.htm

Kratcoski, P. C. (2001). Terrorist victimization: Prevention, control, and recovery. *Studies in Conflict & Terrorism, 24*(6), 467–473. doi:10.1080/105761001753210498

Kurtz, C. F., & Snowden, D. J. (2003). The new dynamics of strategy: Sense making in a complex–complicated world. *IBM Systems Journal, 42*(3), 462–483. Retrieved January 30, 2010, from http://xenia.media.mit.edu/~brooks/storybiz/kurtz.pdf

Lang Jr., A. F. (2010). The politics of punishing terrorists. *Ethics & International Affairs, 24*(1), 3–12.

Langan, P. A., & Levin, D. J. (2002). *Recidivism of prisoners released in 1994.* Retrieved December 4, 2009, from http://bjs.ojp.usdoj.gov/content/pub/pdf/rpr94.pdf

Lefkowitz, J. (2008, May 5). *Terrorists behind bars.* NEFA Foundation.

Lockerbie bomber freed from jail. (2009, August 20). Retrieved December 31, 2009, from http://news.bbc.co.uk/2/hi/uk_news/scotland/south_of_scotland/8197370.stm

Maldives police disperse protest against terrorist as minister. (2008, December 28). *BBC Monitoring South Asia—Political Supplied by BBC Worldwide Monitoring.*

Man questioned in shooting death of Sikh. (2001, September 16). Retrieved October 4, 2010, from http://edition.cnn.com/2001/US/09/16/gen.mesa.shooting/index.html

Margetta, R. (2010, March 4). *Appropriations panel studies request for whole-body scanners at airports.* Retrieved March 27, 2010, from http://www6.lexisnexis.com/publisher/EndUser?Action=UserDisplayFullDocument&orgId=574&topicId=25151&docId=l:1146610883&isRss=true

Marks, A. (2004, March 10). *The impact of '3 strikes' laws a decade later.* Retrieved December 5, 2009, from http://www.csmonitor.com/2004/0310/p02s02-usju.html

Maruna, S. (2001). *Making good: How ex-convicts reform and rebuild their lives.* Washington, D.C.: American Psychological Association.

McCarter, M. (2010, September 13). *Al Qaeda shifts to small attacks, recruiting Americans, report warns.* Retrieved September 15, 2010, from http://www.hstoday.us/content/view/14684/149/

McCauley, C. (2002). Psychological issues in understanding terrorism and the response to terrorism. In C. E. Stout (Ed.), *The Psychology of Terrorism* (pp. 3–29). Westport, Connecticut: Praeger.

McCulloch, J. (2009). Pre-crime and counter-terrorism: Imagining future crime in the 'war on terror' [Abstract]. *British Journal of Criminology, 49*(5) 628–645. doi:10.1093/bjc/azp023

Merari, A. (2005, January). Israel facing terrorism. *Israel Affairs, 11*(1), 223–237. doi:10.1080/1353712042000324535

Moghaddam, F. M. (2006). *From the terrorists' point of view: What they experience and why they come to destroy.* Westport, Connecticut: Praeger Security International.

The Monitor's Editorial Board. (2009, August 24). Compassion in the Lockerbie release. *Christian Science Monitor*, p. 8.

Mulrine, A. (2009, January 13). *Some freed terrorism detainees return to the fight.* Retrieved March 28, 2010, from http://www.usnews.com/news/articles/2009/01/13/some-freed-terrorism-detainees-return-to-the-fight.html

Napolitano stresses shared responsibility. (2009, September 30). Retrieved October 26, 2010, from http://www.upi.com/Business_News/Security-Industry/2009/09/30/Napolitano-stresses-shared-responsibility/UPI-11001254332296/

Napolitano warns chiefs of homegrown threat. (2010, October 26). Retrieved October 26, 2010, from http://www.securityinfowatch.com/printer/1318189?pageNum=1

National sex offender registry. (n.d.). Retrieved November 9, 2010, from http://www.familywatchdog.us/

Neighbour, S. (2009, December 3). Brigitte marked 'never to return'. *The Australian*, p. 3.

Neumann, P. R. (2010). *Prisons and terrorism: Radicalisation and de-radicalisation in 15 countries.* International Centre for the Study of Radicalisation and Political Violence. Retrieved July 14, 2010, from http://www.icsr.info/publications/papers/1277699166PrisonsandTerrorismRadicalisationandDeradicalisationin15Countries

Noricks, D., Helmus, T. C., Paul, C., Berrebi, C., Jackson, B. A., Gvineria, G., . . . & Bahney, B. (2009). In Davis P. K., & Cragin, K. (Eds.), *Social science for counterterrorism: Putting the pieces together.* Santa Monica, California: RAND National Defense Research Institute.

Notice of release and arrival form. (n.d.). Retrieved July 11, 2010, from http://www.bop.gov/policy/forms/Bp_a714.pdf

O'Connell, E., & Benard, C. (2006). A new IO strategy: Prevention and disengagement. *Strategic Insights, V*(5), Retrieved December 5, 2009, from http://www.rand.org/pubs/reprints/2006/RAND_RP1223.pdf

Office of the Director of National Intelligence. (2010). *Summary of the reengagement of detainees formerly held at Guantánamo Bay, Cuba.* Retrieved December 8, 2010, from http://www.dni.gov/electronic_reading_room/120710_Summary_of_the_Reengagement_of_Detainees_Formerly_Held_at_Guantánamo_Bay_Cuba.pdf

Out of the shadows: Getting ahead of prisoner radicalization. (2006, September 19). (Report by the Prisoner Radicalization Task Force.) The George Washington University Homeland Security Policy Institute & The University of Virginia Critical Incident Analysis Group. Retrieved November 12, 2010 from http://www.gwumc.edu/hspi/old/reports/rad/Out%20of%20the%20shadows.pdf

Payne, B. K., & DeMichele, M. (2010, June). The role of probation and parole officers in the collaborative response to sex offenders. *Federal Probation, 74*(1).

Pluchinsky, D. (2008). Global jihadist recidivism: A red flag. *Studies in Conflict & Terrorism, 31*(3), 182–200. doi:10.1080/10576100701878457

Pollack, E. (2010, April 18). *The extremists next door.* Retrieved April 19, 2010, from http://www.nytimes.com/2010/04/19/opinion/19Pollack.html?adxnnl=1&ref=opinion&adxnnlx=1274612669-KNAuRY1NsLZ09CPaTrRuTA

Prison radicalization: Are terrorist cells forming in U.S. cell blocks?: Hearing before the Committee on Homeland Security and Governmental Affairs United States Senate. (S.Hrg. 109-954), 109th Cong. 8 (2006) (testimony of Frank J. Cilluffo).

Probation and pretrial services—mission. (n.d.). Retrieved July 11, 2010, from http://www.uscourts.gov/FederalCourts/ProbationPretrialServices/Mission.aspx

'Proud terrorist' gets life for Trade Center bombing. (1998). Retrieved December 5, 2009, from http://www.cnn.com/US/9801/08/yousef.update/

Quilliam. "About Us." (n.d.). Retrieved December 10, 2010, from http://www.quilliamfoundation.org/about-us.html

Rabasa, A., Pettyjohn, S. L., Ghez, J. J., & Boucek, C. (2010). *Deradicalizing Islamist extremists.* Santa Monica, CA: RAND National Security Research Division. Retrieved December 15, 2010, from http://www.rand.org/pubs/monographs/2010/RAND_MG1053.pdf

Ramo, J. C. (2010). *The age of the unthinkable: Why the new world disorder constantly surprises us and what we can do about it.* New York: Back Bay Books.

Rayda, N. (2009, August 21). *Indonesia's ex-terrorists should be closely watched, say analysts.* Retrieved December 16, 2009, from http://www.thejakartaglobe.com/news/indonesias-ex-terrorists-should-be-closely-watched-say-analysts/325386

Release of Roche 'threat' to public. (2007, May 14). *The Advertiser (Australia),* p. 6.

Rice, D. (2004, March 22). With Britain braced for bombs, we expose an appalling breach of security at airport; terrorist working at Heathrow. *The Express,* p. 14.

Ripley, A., Forster, P., & Thornburgh, N. (2002, October 14). *Do good neighbors make good spies?* Retrieved July 18, 2010, from http://www.time.com/time/magazine/article/0,9171,1003442,00.html

Risk reduction for countering violent extremism. (2010, November). (Exploratory Review by the International Resource Center for Countering Violent Extremism Qatar International Academy for Security Studies (QIASS).

Roche, P. J. (2010, January 25). Why should we shake the hands of reconciliation?; Debate on the meaning of 'forgiveness' and 'reconciliation' in the context of the Troubles is an affront to victims of terrorism. *Belfast Telegraph,* p. 28.

Russo, T. (2010, January 26). The criminal justice system as a counterterrorism tool: A fact sheet. [Web log comment]. Retrieved January 31, 2010, from http://blogs.usdoj.gov/blog/archives/541

Savage, C. (2010, December 21). Detainee review proposal is prepared for Obama. *The New York Times,* p. A19. Retrieved December 21, 2010, from http://www.nytimes.com/2010/12/22/us/22gitmo.html?_r=1&partner=rss&emc=rss

Savage, D. G., & Meyer, J. (2009). *Five alleged 9/11 plotters to be tried in civilian court in New York.* Retrieved December 5, 2009, from http://www.latimes.com/news/nationworld/nation/la-na-gitmo-trials14-2009nov14,0,3018300.story

Sciolino, E., & Schmitt, E. (2008, June 8). *A not very private feud over terrorism.* Retrieved May 26, 2010, from http://www.nytimes.com/2008/06/08/weekinreview/08sciolino.html?_r=4&scp=1&sq=marc+sageman&st=nyt&oref=slogin&oref=slogin

Seifert, K. (2010, Spring). Can Jihadis be rehabilitated? *Middle East Quarterly, XVII*(2), 21–30.

Sherman, J. (2010). *Sessions: Jihadi rehab tied to terror.* Retrieved January 10, 2010, from http://www.politico.com/news/stories/0110/31167.html

Silber, M. D., & Bhatt, A. (2007). *Radicalization in the West: The homegrown threat.* New York City Police Department. Retrieved September 11, 2009, from http://www.nypdshield.org/public/SiteFiles/documents/NYPD_Report-Radicalization_in_the_West.pdf

Singh, J. (2010, January 28). *Parminder Singh Saini detained, Sikhs shocked.* Retrieved March 28, 2010, from http://worldsikhnews.com/27%20January%202010/Parminder%20Singh%20Saini%20detained%20Sikhs%20shocked.htm

Smiles, S., & Knowles, G. (2007, May 18). Roche longs for 'peaceful life' after serving minimum sentence. *The Age (Melbourne, Australia)*, p. 6.

Stern, N. (2010). *Because I say so: The dangerous appeal of moral authority.* Minneapolis, MN: Bascom Hill Books.

Sullivan, M. (2009, October 1). Five Freed terrorists hauled back to jail; fanatic's bid to buy gun. EXCLUSIVE. *The Sun (England)*, p. 17.

Subramanian, S. (2000, April 12). Safeguarding human rights of people in counter terrorist operations. Paper prepared for the *Ancillary Meeting on Terrorist Victimization: Prevention, Control and Recovery.* Vienna: Austria.

Supervision release form. (n.d.). Retrieved July 11, 2010, from http://www.bop.gov/policy/forms/Bp_a0522.pdf

Sutherland, E. H., Cressey, D. R., & Luckenbill, D. F. (1992). *Principles of criminology* (11th ed.). Lanham, Maryland: General Hall.

Swedish court reduces Palestinian terrorist's life sentence. (2008, April 16). Retrieved December 4, 2009, from http://www.haaretz.com/hasen/spages/975654.html

125

Terrorist Expatriation Act. 111th, 2d Cong. (2010). Retrieved May 17, 2010, from
http://lieberman.senate.gov/assets/pdf/TEA_full.pdf

Terrorist freedom fear. (2007, May 14). *Herald Sun (Australia),* p. 11.

Terrorist just wants a quiet life. (2007, May 18). *The Daily Telegraph (Australia)*, p. 19.

Travis, A. (2010, August 27). *Terror warning over radicalised prisoners.* Retrieved
August 27, 2010, from http://www.guardian.co.uk/society/2010/aug/27/radicalised-prisoners-terror-warning

Travis, J. (2006). *But they all come back: facing the challenges of prisoner reentry.*
Washington, D.C.: The Urban Institute Press.

Tucker, D. *Instrumental and organizational approaches to terrorism.* Paper presented at
Naval Postgraduate School, Center for Homeland Defense and Security, Monterey,
California. Unpublished manuscript.

U.S. Department of Justice. National Security Division. (2010). *Introduction to national
security division statistics on unsealed international terrorism and terrorism-related convictions.* Retrieved March 26, 2010, from
http://theplumline.whorunsgov.com/wp-content/uploads/2010/03/March-26-2010-NSD-Final-Statistics.pdf

U.S. Department of Justice, Office of Justice Programs, Bureau of Justice Statistics.
(2007, August 8). Retrieved December 4, 2009, from
http://www.ojp.usdoj.gov/bjs/crimoff.htm#recidivism

U.S.: Scores of Muslim men jailed without charge. (2005, June 27). Retrieved March 28,
2010, from http://www.aclu.org/national-security/us-scores-muslim-men-jailed-without-charge?tab=multimedia

United States intelligence community information sharing strategy. (2008, February 22).
McLean, Virginia: Office of the Director of National Intelligence. Retrieved
December 22, 2010, from
http://www.dni.gov/reports/IC_Information_Sharing_Strategy.pdf

United States v. Comstock et al. No. 08–1224 (United States Supreme Court 2010).
Retrieved May 17, 2010, from http://www.supremecourt.gov/opinions/09pdf/08-1224.pdf

Uniting and Strengthening America by Providing Appropriate Tools Required to
Intercept and Obstruct Terrorism (USA PATRIOT ACT) Act of 2001, Pub. L. 107-56, 115 Stat. 272, H.R. 3162, enacted October 26, 2001. (2001). Retrieved
December 7, 2010, from http://www.gpo.gov/fdsys/pkg/PLAW-107publ56/pdf/PLAW-107publ56.pdf

Uniting and Strengthening America by Providing Appropriate Tools Required to Intercept and Obstruct Terrorism (USA PATRIOT ACT) Act of 2001, § 3583(j)U.S.C. TITLE 18 > PART II > CHAPTER 227 > SUBCHAPTER D. (2001). Retrieved December 7, 2010 from http://frwebgate.access.gpo.gov/cgi-bin/getdoc.cgi?dbname=107_cong_public_laws&docid=f:publ056.107

USA Today. (Editorial). (2009, December 4). *Huckabee's pardonable error.* Retrieved December 4, 2009, from http://blogs.usatoday.com/oped/2009/12/our-opinion-on-men-in-trouble-huckabees-pardonable-error.html#more

Violent Crime Control and Law Enforcement Act of 1994. (1994). Retrieved July 11, 2010, from http://frwebgate.access.gpo.gov/cgi-bin/getdoc.cgi?dbname=103_cong_bills&docid=f:h3355enr.txt.pdf

Wan, W. (2010, October 28). *Sting underscores Muslims' complex relationship with FBI.* Retrieved October 29, 2010, from http://www.washingtonpost.com/wp-dyn/content/article/2010/10/28/AR2010102806320.html?hpid=topnews

What is the Office for Victims of Crime? (2010, April). Retrieved September 14, 2010, from http://www.ovc.gov/publications/factshts/what_is_OVC2010/intro.html#rtm

Whoriskey, P., & Eggen, D. (2008, January 23). *Judge sentences Padilla to 17 years, cites his detention.* Retrieved September 22, 2010, from http://www.washingtonpost.com/wp-dyn/content/article/2008/01/22/AR2008012200565.html

Williams, C. J. (2007, December 31). *Guantánamo Bay detainee, 68, dies of cancer.* Retrieved March 28, 2010, from http://articles.latimes.com/2007/dec/31/nation/na-gitmo31

Wolf, F. (2009). In Obama B. (Ed.), *Letter regarding release of six Guantánamo Bay detainees to Yemen.*

Wright, R. G. (2008, March 5). Sex offender post-incarceration sanctions: Are there any limits? *New England Journal on Criminal and Civil Confinement, 34*(17), 17–50.

Yemen parcel bombmaker believed to be Al Qaeda terrorist Ibrahim Hassan Al Isiri. (2010, October 30). Retrieved October 31, 2010, from http://www.telegraph.co.uk/news/worldnews/middleeast/yemen/8099241/Yemen-parcel-bombmaker-believed-to-be-al-Qaeda-terrorist-Ibrahim-Hassan-Al-Asiri.html

Zabel, R. B., & Benjamin, J. J. (2008, May). *In pursuit of justice: prosecuting terrorism cases in the federal courts.* New York, NY: Human Rights First.

Zabel, R. B., & Benjamin, J. J. (2009, July). *In pursuit of justice: prosecuting terrorism cases in the federal courts, 2009 update and recent developments.* New York, NY: Human Rights First.

Zimbardo, P. G. (2007). *The Lucifer effect: Understanding how good people turn evil.* New York, NY: Random House.